CW00746148

Parramón Handbooks

MIXING COLOURS OILS

Parramón Handbooks

MIXING
COLOURS
OILS

Ⓟ Parramón

CONTENTS

CONTENTS

INTRODUCTION

In Search of Color

Man has always attempted to represent the reality of what he has observed. Depicting realistically what he saw or imagined (sacred art), he limited himself to depicting subjects using only colors of the real world. Nowadays, painters can choose any range of colors to interpret what they see, even if those colors do not coincide with those of the model before them. Furthermore, painters can use colors to create visual and sensorial stimuli in the form of abstract art.

Whatever the case, the artist must have an idea of the color scheme he wants to work with before commencing a picture. More often than not, the exact color of the model that the artist wishes to paint cannot be purchased as such. Therefore, he is compelled to create it.

of color is nothing more than the result of mixtures of certain colors.

Palette Work

Oil painters create their mixtures as they work, either on the palette or directly on the canvas. If necessary, the mixture can be modified, since it is often difficult to obtain the exact proportions the first time. Adding a touch more of one color to a mixture results in an entirely new mix, because it acquires a different hue. The painter does this constantly as he develops his painting.

Reference Point

To create the right mixture, it is necessary to have a reference point. All

quantities. You should bear in mind that it is impossible to indicate the exact proportions of each color required to obtain the mixture in a way that would be useful for the painter. To determine what colors to use, and how much of each one, the artist needs some basic knowledge of how to achieve the desired colors that he can put into practice.

Theory in Practice

The research into the nature of light and color carried out by Isaac Newton (1642–1727), Thomas Young (1773–1829) and Wilhelm Ostwald (1853–1932), and others, provided artists with a methodology to work with. Color theory applied to the oil medium is useful for obtaining pigment colors, secondary colors, and tertiary colors from primary colors. Because of the characteristics of oil colors, neutral colors can be mixed that, in their darkest ranges, are dull and somewhat "gray," and become even grayer if white is added. In this way, we can obtain over 90 percent of colors.

The advantage of understanding color theory allows the artist to paint in a methodical manner. It is highly useful to know which colors are required for the mixture and in what proportions.

All the mixtures that you see on this palette were produced during a single painting session. Sometimes the artist finds it necessary to clean the palette more than once as the work progresses.

Oil:
Application and Mix

A painting requires an almost infinite number of colors and tones, applied by superimposing or juxtaposing them, as well as by utilizing all the other techniques and materials that this medium offers. The key to a successful oil painting is a sound knowledge of how to obtain correct color mixtures. The mixture is applied with a brush, a palette knife, a finger, or as a glaze, and should be related to the other colors in accordance to the composition and structure of the painting. In short, a specific area

oil paint brands manufacture products that, although they may differ in value and quality, are sold as standard colors. More information on this aspect of pigment colors is provided on the following pages.

What Colors?
How Much of Each One?

When we want to obtain a color mixture, we must decide what colors we are going to use to produce it and in what

The Value of Experience

Experience in palette work is essential, because it gives us an idea about the limitations of subtractive synthesis; it demonstrates the convenience of using pigment colors rather than the primary colors; and it reveals the problems that can arise when adding white to a mixture, since in addition to lightening the color, it can also "gray" it. Hands-on experience is the only way to master the art of mixing colors.

Introduction
How to Use the Handbook
Color Theory: What Is Color?

7

HOW TO USE THE HANDBOOK

Procedure

The book is based on practical exercises that put the theories explained into practice. The first section of exercises shows how it is possible to paint a picture with only three colors plus white. Palette work is taught by practical demonstrations of the chromatic characteristics of each one of the standard colors, that is, commercially manufactured colors. The procedure is simple and gradual: Before explaining more complex mixtures, we will first examine what can be achieved with the most basic ones.

Thus, the reader gradually learns the effects produced by mixing one color with another and discovers the properties that those colors can lend a mixture. In this way, she is able to work out which color will be most appropriate for a determined mixture, and which one will be least suitable to be included.

Ostwald saw colors as having temperature, a theory that supports our current color ranges and is used to develop color harmonization in the field of painting, of which the two most important subjects are complement and contrast.

It is equally important to observe the colors of reality. Such an analysis can provide the artist with ways of painting volume and conveying atmosphere through color.

Finally, the *Atlas of Colors* by Harald Küppers and the Computerized Chromatic Wheel, among others, are two sources that are of great help to the painter for reference purposes.

Using the Handbook

Books concerned with the subject of oil color mixtures are only useful if accompanied by practical demonstrations. The aim of this book is to show the reader how to obtain specific color mixtures. We will use the oil medium and its techniques to explain general color theory. The colors are introduced gradually and in the most practical way, while at the same time providing the reader with the basics of color theory, as well as rules, advice, hints, guidelines, and so forth.

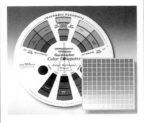

The Atlas of Colors *by Küppers and the Computerized Chromatic Wheel.*

Key

Abbreviations. For the sake of simplicity, the colors mentioned are abbreviated. See the chart below.

The + sign. This is placed between the abbreviations of two colors to indicate that both must be mixed in equal quantities.

Pantone colors. This type of colors has been selected in order to allow the reader to see which standard colors the abbreviations belong to.

The sign —— Ex.: <u>CYL + RM</u>
↓   ↓
                    red

This indicates that by mixing the two standard colors CYL (cadmium yellow lemon) and RM (rose madder) in equal parts we obtain red.

Practicality. This system allows the reader to rapidly identify the colors required without having to repeat the complete names every time.

The system's limitations. In theory, it is possible to create mixtures of colors in equal parts. In practice, however, measurements are merely approximations. In the section concerned with procedures, you will see that with experience it is possible to obtain the right amounts through rough measurements.

"Plenty of," "just a hint of," "a little." As we mentioned earlier, it is not possible to formulate precise measurements for obtaining color mixtures. Therefore we are compelled to resort to terms such as "plenty of," "slightly less," "very little." This is the best way of describing the amounts of color required to obtain a determined mix.

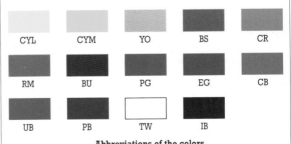

Abbreviations of the colors

CYL = Cadmium yellow lemon	PG = Permanent green
CYM = Cadmium yellow medium	EG = Emerald green
YO = Yellow ochre	CB = Cobalt blue
BS = Burnt sienna	UB = Ultramarine blue
CR = Cadmium red	PB = Prussian blue
RM = Rose madder	TW = Titanium white
BU = Burnt umber	IB = Ivory black

8

How to Use the Handbook
Color Theory: What Is Color?
Additive Synthesis and Subtractive Synthesis

COLOR THEORY: WHAT IS COLOR?

A Fundamental Question for the Artist

"What is color?" is a complex question, and it has a complex answer. A book with a blue cover is a book with a blue cover. The book does not change, it simply is what it is. But its blue characteristic can be perceived by people, by means of their sense of sight, only when the object is exposed to light, be it daylight or artificial light. Color can exist only if light reaches the object and a human eye is present to perceive it.

First Studies on Light

The experiments on light carried out by Isaac Newton and Thomas Young established several fundamental principles. The most important of these is that light is color. Newton broke down light into a spectrum of seven colors.

Young did exactly the opposite. He established his principle by reconstructing light. From this experiment Young deduced that the seven colors of the spectrum discovered by Newton could be reduced to three colors: dark blue, intense red, and intense green. The result of superimposing three light

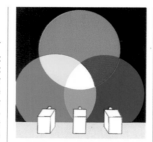

A representation of Young's experiment.

beams of each of these colors was white light.

Absorption and Reflection

Why do objects have colors? Thanks to Young we know that white light is composed of a beam of three colored lights. When white light illuminates an object, the object absorbs some of the colors and reflects the others. The color reflected by the object is its own. The principle of absorption and reflection of light states that when any opaque body is illuminated, it reflects all or part of the components of the light it receives: 1. White bodies reflect all colors; 2. Black colors absorb all colors; 3. Gray objects absorb and reflect equal amounts

of red, green, and dark blue; 4. Yellow objects absorb dark blue and reflect red and green; 5. Magenta objects reflect dark blue and red and absorb green; 6. A cyan blue surface absorbs red and reflects dark blue and green.

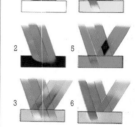

A graphic representation of the way light is absorbed or reflected on colored bodies.
1. White bodies reflect all colors;
2. Black colors absorb all colors;
3. Gray objects absorb and reflect equal amounts of red, green, and dark blue; 4. Yellow objects absorb dark blue and reflect red and green; 5. A magenta object reflects dark blue and red and absorbs green; 6. A cyan blue surface absorbs red and reflects dark blue and green.

So, What Is Color?

First, color is the sensory effect produced by the human eye when the retina receives light of different wavelengths (between 400 and 760 nanometers).

Second, due to the principle of reflection and refraction of light, color is a property of objects according to how they are seen in daylight.

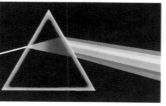

400	450	480	560	590	760
1	2	3	4	5	6

A representation of Newton's experiment: A beam of light shone through a triangular prism is dispersed into seven colors of the spectrum.

The color wavelength corresponds to the color spectrum as seen and produced by the retina: 1. intense blue; 2. blue; 3. green; 4. yellow; 5. red; 6. purple.

ADDITIVE SYNTHESIS AND SUBTRACTIVE SYNTHESIS

Additive Synthesis: "Light" Colors

Additive synthesis is the direct consequence of the principle of absorption and reflection of light. From a beam of white light it is possible to obtain "light" colors, that is, the colors of light. Closer observation of this spectrum reveals that there are primary and secondary light colors.

Additive Synthesis

White is obtained by superimposing the three primary colors: green, red, and dark blue (see Figure A1).

If we superimpose two primary light colors, we obtain the secondary light colors: yellow from superimposing the light colors red and green (2); magenta from red and dark blue (3); cyan blue from dark blue and green (4).

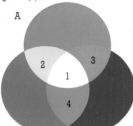

This diagram shows the result produced by mixing light colors together. White light is created when the three primary light colors are superimposed over one another. When two primary light colors are superimposed, they produce secondary colors: yellow, magenta, and cyan blue.

Complementary Light Colors

Red and green produce yellow, which is the complementary light color of dark blue. The other two complementary pairs are: magenta and green, and cyan blue and red.

Subtractive Synthesis: Pigment Colors

Physicists work with light colors; painters, on the other hand, work with pigment colors. Pigment colors are solid colors that can be applied on a surface. They are made up of pigment and binder. The type of binder depends on the pictorial medium: Oils require rectified linseed oil to bind the pigment together. Pigment colors can be transparent, semi-opaque, or opaque. With pigment colors the artist paints by subtractive synthesis, establishing suitable relationships between pigment color primaries and secondaries.

Subtractive Synthesis

Black is produced when the three primary pigment colors—yellow, magenta, and cyan blue—are mixed together (see figure B1). By mixing yellow and magenta together, we obtain red (2); magenta and cyan blue produce dark blue (3); cyan blue and yellow produce green (4). (Cyan blue, a light blue, is used in graphic arts.)

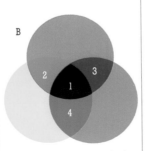

This diagram shows the result of mixtures between pigment colors. Black is created when all three pigment colors are mixed together. By mixing yellow and magenta you obtain red. Yellow and cyan blue produce green. Finally, magenta and cyan blue produce a darker blue.

Complementary Pigment Colors

When the primary pigment colors (P) magenta and cyan blue are mixed, you obtain the secondary (S) dark blue, whose complement is the primary color (P) that was not included in the mixture (yellow). Using the same procedure, you can see that dark blue is the complement of yellow (1); red is the complement of cyan blue (2); and green is the complement of magenta (3); and vice versa.

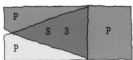

Graphic examples of the effects of complementary pigment colors.

To Avoid Confusion

• The primary pigment colors are the secondary light colors, and the secondary pigment colors are the primary light colors.

• Whenever oil mixtures are mentioned, we are referring to pigment colors.

• The painter who wishes to reproduce what he sees or has in mind with oil paints does this by subtracting light, in other words, by subtractive synthesis.

CLASSIFICATION OF PIGMENT COLORS

Primary, Secondary, and Tertiary Colors

By mixing the three primary pigment colors in pairs of equal parts, we obtain the secondary colors. The tertiary colors are produced by mixing a primary color with the closest secondary color in equal parts. In total, there are three primary colors, three secondary colors, and six tertiary colors. Any two colors that are diametrically opposed in the color wheel are called complementary colors. The colors adjacent to the complementary color are known as indirect complementaries.

Temperature and Color

Wilhelm Ostwald's theory on color (1916) is highly practical. It remains relevant to painters to this day. He divided colors into warm and cool types. Artists made practical use of his theories by creating various **classified** color ranges. This classification, however, could not include less defined colors.

Psychological Associations

Psychology and color. Warm and cool colors are related to the sensation (psychological association) an individual feels on seeing them. Even though certain reaction patterns have been identified with colors by psychological association, such experiences are highly subjective.

Symbolism of colors. Yellow is associated with health and power; red with passion, strength, and pomposity; blue with coldness, pureness, and intelligence; pink with benevolence; orange with joy, concentration, and intimacy; white with purity, naiveté, and serenity; and violet with gratitude.

Tone of colors and their expressive connotations. A diffuse and subdued harmony of colors (such as pastel colors) creates an ethereal and mellow atmosphere. A specific set of highly contrasted intense tones gives rise to an energetic and dynamic atmosphere, which could even be characterized as harsh.

Classification of Colors by Temperature

Warm colors. Warm colors produce the sensation of heat, proximity, and grandeur. Warm colors comprise all the ranges between magenta and yellow, including the adjacent colors of the chromatic wheel: carmine and red, orange and orange-yellow, yellow, ochre, earth colors, violet, violet-blue, and greenish yellows. Decreasing saturation and luminosity cool warm colors down.

Cool colors. These colors tend to convey coldness and distance. They range from green to blue, with the limits from yellow-green to violet-blue. Other cool colors include gray tones of bluish, greenish, and neutral tendencies. Less saturated cool colors appear warmer than the very intense ones.

Neutral colors. A neutral color is obtained by mixing two complementary colors together in unequal proportions with or without the addition of white. Therefore, the characteristic feature of a neutral color is a tone of a grayish tendency. (When the complementary colors are mixed together in equal parts they produce black.) Neutral colors can take on a warm or cool tendency. It can be said that neutral colors appear dirty when compared with ordinary warm and cool colors.

Additional information. Yellowish-green tones can acquire a warm or cool tendency. The same goes for violet-blue tones. Ochres and earth tones are warm but neutral. When the painter works with unsaturated colors or mixtures, the temperature of the applications is always a *referential deduction*, arrived at by comparing one color with another.

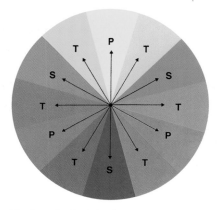

*The chromatic wheel, classification of pigment colors:
P = primary, S = secondary, T = tertiary.
The mixing of 2 Ps produces an S. The mixing of one P with the
closest of each S produces the Ts (in total 3 Ps, 3 Ss and 6 Ts).*

PLANNING A PAINTING: THE COLORS

Painting Is Not a Science

First we choose our subject. Then we study it and decide on the most suitable composition and structure. Finally, we choose a general color scheme. The artist must try to see the color mixtures he will use as a whole; in other words, they must be related to one another.

To seek a harmony is to look for the optimum correspondence of one color with the others. Such a task is intuitive and very personal.

Since painting is often instinctive and impulsive, the artist should not repress his feelings. Therefore, all artists must find their own balance between mastering painting techniques (which requires study and practice and is not generally creative) and freeing themselves from influences in order to paint with spontaneity, even if that means sometimes breaking the rules.

Color ranges

The application of different color ranges increases our sensitivity and widens considerably the possibility of achieving complex and personalized color and tonal associations.

What is range? In painting, range is any succession of ordered colors or tones. The order of colors of a spectrum is a range or complete series. The following ranges are the ones most commonly used.

Simple Ranges. The *melodic range* is composed of a single color, broken down into two different tones, and includes black and white.

The *simple harmonic range* is composed of a predominant color, its complementary, and two more colors, situated opposite to the complementary color.

Free brushwork using only one color, magenta, mixed with white and a blackish tone.

The complete range: harmonic range of warm colors, cool colors, and neutral colors.

1. Harmonic range of warm colors (the work contains an obvious predominance of warm colors);

Diagram of the simple harmonic range.

2. Harmonic range of cool colors (the work contains a clear predominance of cool colors);

3. Harmonic range of neutral colors (composed of pairs of colors in unequal proportions, grayish, or lacking white).

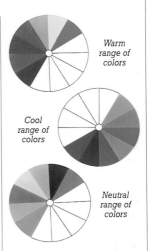

Warm range of colors

Cool range of colors

Neutral range of colors

Contrast and Induction Factors

Regardless of the range you choose to paint with, it is essential to bear in mind contrast and induction factors.

Contrast Through Tone and Color

A color appears darker when the color around it is lighter. Inversely, a color appears lighter when the color around it is darker.

Contrast through tone: By painting a light tone next to a dark tone, the light tone appears lighter and the dark tone appears darker.

Maximum contrast: By painting a color next to its complementary color in their most intense tones, you obtain a maximum color contrast through tone and through color.

Induction of Complementary Colors

A color will cast its complementary color onto an adjacent color. In practice, a brushstroke of color applied on canvas acquires some of its complementary color due to the effect of the surrounding color.

LEARNING TO OBSERVE: ANALYSIS FROM NATURE

Light changes throughout the day.

Learning to Observe: Light

How do we study light? We know that without light there can be no color, so we should begin with a systematic study of the effects of light on the bodies it comes into contact with.

Characteristics of light. The color of an object depends on the nature of light that is illuminating it. It is important to observe light and know how to describe it. First we must establish the type of light: natural (sunlight, moonlight) or artificial (electric light, fluorescent gas, candlelight), as well as its origin, quality, localization, and intensity.

Learning to Observe: The Atmosphere

Regardless of the subject we choose to paint, all the objects contained within it should be regarded as a whole in which there exist different planes. The foreground is noticeably contrasted and sharp in comparison with the more distant planes.

We normally distinguish planes as the foreground, the middle ground, and the background. A landscape may contain all three, two, or only one. The still life normally has two: the foreground and the immediate background.

It is important to decide how much prominence you want to give each component within the whole and how much definition it requires, since the rest of the work will hinge on your decision.

It is easy to see the different planes, which can be differentiated between those with contrast and sharpness and those that are fuzzier and grayish.

Learning to Observe: The Color of Objects

Once you have established the type of light and the surrounding atmosphere, you should bear in mind that, to a greater or lesser extent, all illuminated subjects have three color factors: 1. the local color, or the object's own specific color; 2. the tonal color, that is, the color variations that result from the effects of light and shadow; 3. the color of the environment, or the color reflected by other surrounding objects or elements.

This tree shows the characteristics of light: the local color, tonal color, and color of the environment; the chromaticity of the shadow it casts; the greater contrast and sharpness of the middle ground compared with the background.

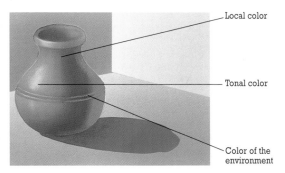

Local color

Tonal color

Color of the environment

An orange vase with three colors (the local color, the tonal, and the color of the environment), situated on a blue plane.

Learning to Observe: The Color of Shadows

It is important to differentiate between the part of the object in shadow and the part cast by the object. The reference color of the object's shadow is the color of the object itself. Note at the edge of an object's own shadow the presence of additional light—the reflection originating from a second object.

The shadow cast by the object also contains a reflection from a nearby object. In all shadows cast by an object we can observe the distorted shape of the object itself. Furthermore, within this shape, we can distinguish various zones that accord with local color, tonal color, and color of the environment, which in this case is related to the second object.

It is essential to establish a good relationship between the colors of the object (local, tonal, and environmental) and the colors of its shadow.

How do you paint the color of shadows? The color of any shadow is a mixture of blue (characteristic of darkness), the local color in a darker tone, which is in turn mixed with the complementary of that local color. Certain painting schools place greater emphasis on the complementary color.

Learning to Observe: Adjusting the Painting

A painting is said to be well-adjusted when the maximum interrelationships between the colors of the objects and their respective shadows have been achieved. This adjustment should be carried out in compliance with the color range the artist has chosen to paint in.

Every object has its local color, tonal color, and color of its environment, plus the respective shadows cast with their local color, tonal color, and color of the environment. Note, in addition, how the shadow of one of the objects is partially cast over the other one.

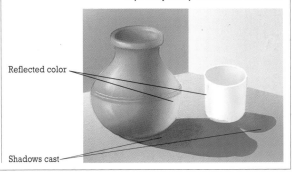

Reflected color

Shadows cast

THE OIL MEDIUM AND ITS MATERIALS

Medium: Drying

An oil painting is executed by superimposing layers of paint with successive approximations to the final colors. In general a picture is painted over several sessions because oil paint dries slowly.

The oil paint medium (oil) dries by means of oxidation, when it comes into contact with the air. The drying process takes place gradually, from the uppermost layer down to the very first application. In order to ensure that the painting dries properly (so that it doesn't crack later on), it is essential to follow the rule of "fat over lean." The first layer should be applied "lean." The painter therefore requires only the minimum of materials.

The Materials

• **Refined linseed oil** is one of the basic components of oil paint; it is a fatty medium. Another fatty medium is **walnut oil.**

• **Rectified turpentine** acts as a solvent to linseed oil; it's a lean medium.

• **Unrectified turpentine** is not suitable for use in painting; it is better left for cleaning brushes.

• **Tubes of oil paint.** Oil paint is composed of an oily medium (linseed oil) and pigment color.

• **Palette, brushes, palette**

The colors on the palette: The cool colors have been placed vertically from top to bottom along the left-hand side of the palette, while the warm ones have been arranged left to right across the top according to their "temperature." Another common arrangement consists of situating the paints from left to right along the top, arranging them from warm to cool.

knife, palette cups, and **supports.**

• **Turpentine, cotton rags, kitchen towels,** and **newspaper.**

Remember

• Palette cups are essential. They are available individually and in pairs. The paired type can be used for two purposes: one is filled with turpentine, to be used for cleaning the brushes while you paint; the other is filled with roughly 60% linseed oil and 40% turpentine, and used to apply the lean layers of paint.

Some painters use just one cup for the solution and a jar filled with turpentine for cleaning the brushes. Even though it is cheaper than rectified turpentine, unrectified turpentine ruins both the brushes and the oil paint.

• The way in which the artist arranges the colors on his palette allows him to easily locate a color. The colors should normally be arranged in their different ranges, that is, in cool, warm, and neutral ranges. Many painters situate a large quantity of white on the palette, always in the same place.

Palette, slab for the oil paste, palette knives, paints, palette cups, supports (canvas, wood, cardboard, and paper), refined linseed oil, rectified turpentine, unrectified turpentine, cotton rags and cloths.

OIL: TECHNIQUES

The First Application

It is essential to apply the first layer of paint correctly on the canvas, in order for the paint to adhere properly and to dry so that it does not crack over time. The painter can go about this task in various ways:

• She can apply a layer of "lean," a diluted layer of paint. This color or color mixture is diluted by adding some of the solution mentioned earlier, which contains turpentine mixed with linseed oil.

It should be so thin that it trickles down the canvas.

• It is also possible to apply a completely lean layer using latex or acrylic paint. These are aqueous lean media that dry fast and allow you to then continue painting over in oil, during the very same session.

When is the first application dry enough to paint over? If the first layer is applied with diluted paint, you will have to wait for it to dry before continuing. A couple of days is the normal time it takes to dry. If you don't wait, the colors applied on top will mix with the underlying layer, thus dirtying both layers.

The best way of confirming that it is dry is by pressing your fingertip on to the application; if, on removing it, there is no trace of paint on your finger, you can proceed with the second layer (even if the paint feels sticky to the touch). Carry out this test in

several places around the canvas, because the application may not be uniform: Different colors and/or different thicknesses take more or less time to dry.

The same test should be carried out even when you apply latex or acrylic. When dealing with two media, a water-based one and an oil-based one, the latter won't adhere properly if the former hasn't dried thoroughly.

Loading some solvent onto the brush.

The Second Layer

When painting with a brush, the second layer should be mixed with some of the solution from the palette cup: Dip the brush in the mixture and then load some paint onto it, making a circular movement. It is easy to see the change in the density of the paint. By applying it on the canvas, you will see how the paint spreads more easily.

The amount of this mixture you use with the paint should be slightly reduced with every new layer.

Final Layers and Retouching

The final layers and the retouches are applied without altering the density of the paint; that is, they are applied straight from the tubes or from your palette.

Example of an initial application.

SELECTION OF PIGMENT COLORS

An Open Method

Standard colors can be used as a reference source in terms of mixtures and results. All manufactured oil color brands, with varying shades and qualities, are sold as standard colors.

It is not practical to work with too many colors at the same time. Furthermore, it is unrealistic to speak of a universal palette. There are countless options and all of them are equally valid. Starting from this premise, this book provides an open method.

Any standard color that is not mentioned can be incorporated into its corresponding group and its chromatic characteristics can be studied by following the same guidelines set out in the following pages.

Likewise, given that the results and proportions of the mixtures depend directly on their capacity to alter the colors that are combined with them, each painter should get to know the characteristics of his personalized palette.

Experimenting with Standard Colors

Titanium white. This is the most commonly used type of white. Its drying time and opacity is highly suitable for painting in general. Other whites are silver white (highly toxic, very opaque, fast-drying, and liable to crack),

Example of a Color and Its Characteristics

Explanation of the signs:
★★★ *Degree of permanency*
506 *Number classification in the standard color chart*
□ *Transparent color*
2 *Price group reference*
PB 29 *Pigment composition*

Ultramarine blue deep
★★★ 506 □ 2
PB 29

General Meaning

Permanency:
★★★ *Maximum degree*
★★ *Good degree*

Opacity-transparency sign:
□ *Transparent*
■ *Opaque*
▨ *Semi-opaque*
▧ *Semi-transparent*

and zinc white (less opaque, but very slow-drying).

Ivory black. This is a deep black. Depending on the brand, it can have a warm shade. Most painters rarely use black in their blends. When used to paint a specific area, ivory black is favored over lamp black, since the latter has less covering power.

Yellows

Cadmium yellow lemon, cadmium yellow medium. These are brilliant and potent colors. Of all the yellows, these take the longest to dry, but many painters prefer them to Naples yellow and chrome yellow, which are highly toxic.

Yellow ochre. This earth color has excellent covering power.

Reds

Burnt sienna. Raw sienna is the most earthy of the yellows, and burnt sienna is the reddest of the red earth tones. It is important to bear in mind that this color has a tendency to blacken.

Cadmium red. Because vermilion dries slowly and is sensitive to light, painters opt for cadmium red, which, though not as bright, is potent, and far more permanent. The lacquers have a highly luminous finish. It is essential to study the behavior of each red that you want to include on your palette.

Rose madder. This is a very intense red, which can be used to obtain a wide range of tones. It has a great capacity of transparency when required.

Browns

Burnt umber. As its name indicates, it derives from an earth product. It should be applied with care because it tends to blacken and dries very quickly. It is preferable to Van Dyck, which cracks easily.

Greens

Permanent green. It is warm and luminous. As its name suggests, it is resistant to light. This green is very opaque.

Emerald green. It is an intense color. It has notable transparent possibilities.

Blues

Cobalt blue deep, Prussian blue, ultramarine blue deep. Three blues of very different chromatic qualities. They are made from natural or artificial substances (imitating lapis lazuli). Cobalt blue does produce cracking. Ultramarine blue deep is transparent and has a medium-drying capacity. Prussian blue is an intense color that can dominate other colors. It can also produce very transparent shades. It is best to have one or two dark blues and a cerulean.

Other Colors: Learning About a New Color

When you decide to incorporate a new color into your palette, it is important to think about the effect it will have on the color groups: the yellows, reds, greens, blues, and earth colors (neutral colors).

The painter's tendency toward a specific range may persuade him to broaden his palette with other colors, or even reduce them. You may, for example, include a **transparent earth pink** in your palette.

The decision to add a good **violet** would be suitable for heightening the range of violets. An alternative would be to use a tertiary color, in this case, a mix of blue and rose madder. Some artists do not use many greens in their paintings. For instance, there is no need to resort to **permanent green** since it can be produced by mixing the other colors of the palette; similarly, a landscape artist might do the same in order to obtain **cerulean blue** for his painting.

Information on Paints

All reasonable quality paint brands include information on their products. The label on the tube supplies certain details, while in other cases you may have to consult the manufacturer's color chart. It is important to study this information before you purchase your paints.

Permanency. Most brands of oil paints indicate the paint's permanency or resistance to light with stars (asterisks) or plus signs. The colors most resistant to light are indicated with three or four such symbols (+++; ****) if, for instance, the manufacturer uses these codes.

Opacity and transparency. One important item of information is the reference to the color's opacity or transparency.

Whether the manufacturer uses a square or a circle (or another symbol), an empty box or circle means transparency, a split-box or circle indicates semi-transparency, a half-filled box or circle indicates semi-opacity, and a filled box or circle indicates opacity. This is important to know when mixing colors and creating glazes.

Content. Other information provided on tubes of oil paints includes the amount of pigments and oxide contained in them. Such information is important because, for instance, colors that contain cadmium (yellow, red) are intense, mixable, and permanent; this type tends to be expensive.

Some brands offer alternative colors manufactured by modifying their formula, and sold at more accessible prices. It is advisable to have a good yellow and a good red. Mixing them with other colors of the palette creates more luminous and cleaner colors.

VARIOUS TECHNIQUES

How to Mix Colors

The painter's personality is reflected in her work, in the materials she employs (those things she has acquired over time), and in the way she mixes her colors.

Purists prefer to apply their completely mixed colors (having made the mixture on the palette) thickly on the canvas. Others partially mix their colors on the palette and finish the job on the canvas, blending them into previously applied layers of color.

Painters who do not mix their colors on the palette paint with color directly from the tube or from colors previously mixed on the palette. They apply the paint in thick impasto, with few brushstrokes and brush movements. In this kind of painting, we can see how filaments of one color mix with the other. By working with a palette knife, the artist can apply paint directly from the tube or colors previously mixed on the palette. The mixtures can be applied by painting impasto, in streaks, by sgraffito, or by pointillism. Some painters use all the techniques, depending on what they want to achieve.

The variety of mixing techniques depends on:

• The instruments used and their effects on the resulting mixtures.
• The homogeneity of a color mixture.

To summarize, regardless of the technique chosen, we attain the desired goal: a color mixture.

Color Technique Procedures

There are various ways of mixing colors depending on:
• The implement used: a) palette knife, b) brush, c) finger (special case)
• The surface on which they are to be mixed: a) palette, b) the canvas or other support.

The technique can be divided up into three specific phases:
1. Separating the amounts of color required for the mixture (using a palette knife or a brush; it is normally done on the palette).
2. Blending the colors to obtain the desired mixture (in general this is carried out on the palette, but it can be done on the canvas).
3. Applying the color to the canvas or other support.

The order can alter, depending on the painter's habits.

Degree of Color: Homogeneity of a Color Mixture

• A high grade mixture is one in which the colors are totally mixed together.
• A low grade mixture is an optical mix, that is, when two pure colors are juxtaposed or loosely scrambled on the canvas (as in impressionism and pointillism).

There are a number of variations between these two extremes.

Remember

• Don't add any solvent when you are mixing the colors on the palette. This is done when the paint is applied on the canvas.
• Always remember to paint fat over lean.
• Make sure you have the most basic colors to start painting, and arrange them on the palette according to their "temperature."

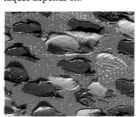

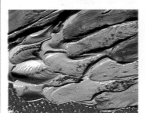

Different degrees of homogeneity of a color mix.

PALETTE KNIFE TECHNIQUES

The Palette Knife

This is an essential tool for mixing your colors on the palette. The palette knife is also used to measure and dose the paint.

A medium-size palette knife is the most appropriate for mixing colors. It shouldn't be too long, too short, too wide, or too narrow. Make sure the tip is not too round.

Mixing the Colors on the Palette

Mixing colors directly on the support requires plenty of experience and practice. The best way to learn is to start by mixing them on the palette. More information about how to do this is provided on page 22.

Different types of palette knives. They serve many purposes: for cleaning the palette, for painting, for mixing, etc.

Depositing the color in an area of the palette.

Scooping an amount (a rough measurement) of paint onto the palette knife.

First Step: Preparing the Colors for a Mixture

Scoop up a quantity of paint onto the palette knife from the deposits of paint arranged around the edge of your palette. Then place it in a clean area of the palette. Regardless of whether you use the top or bottom part of the palette knife, the paint is deposited by pressing it on the palette so it sticks there. Try to deposit as much of the paint from the palette knife as possible. Now clean the knife with a cotton rag or piece of newspaper to remove all the remaining paint.

Repeat the operation again with the next color, scooping up the amount you consider necessary to obtain the right blend.

If your mixture requires only two colors, place them next to each other, leaving a gap in between them to mix the two together. If the mixture requires three colors, place them in a circle.

Cleanliness

It is essential to clean the palette knife every time you scoop up a new color. There are two good reasons for doing this: first, so you can judge better the small quantities of paint and, second, to prevent dirtying the main deposits of color arranged around the palette. Each painter has her own idea of how clean she wants to keep her palette.

b

a

*Two examples of how the colors are arranged before mixing them:
a. of two colors
b. of three colors*

PALETTE KNIFE TECHNIQUES: MIXING

Second Step: Mixing with the Palette Knife

To obtain the mixture, the palette knife must be dragged in circular movements to bind the colors together. It is not only a question of mixing two specific quantities of paint, but also of blending tiny proportions of the colors to achieve the exact hue the artist is searching for.

• There are mixtures that require similar amounts of each color. They are mixed together in a neutral zone, adding rough quantities. The artist should observe the first result and then add a little of one or the other colors in order to obtain the right shade.

• When a very tiny amount of one color is required in a mixture (as compared to the amount of other colors to be included), more care must be taken. If too much of the minority color is added, the painter will be forced to compensate for his error by adding large amounts of the dominant color(s) to readjust the mixture.

You should begin with a very tiny proportion of the color, and mix it in an area separate from but close to the edge of the dominant color. Then start mixing and adding more of the dominant color until you achieve the right

Painting with the palette knife.

mixture. This is done by dragging tiny amounts of the dominant color to the mixing zone.

General Rule

• When a standard color is to be used as the dominant color in a mixture, you should begin with a very tiny amount of the other color. Then gradually add a quantity of the dominant color to the mixture.

• If the mixture doesn't turn out as expected, or if it becomes dirty, start over. Clean the imple-

ments thoroughly. Before starting again, try to see if the mistake was theoretical or if it was due to the technique you used.

Third Step: Applying the Paint to the Canvas

The palette knife can also be used to apply paint onto the canvas while the previously painted colors are still wet. The knife allows the artist to execute very uniform mixtures.

General Rule

• It is advisable to use the palette knife to paint with when you want to apply large quantities of homogenous mixtures.

Mixing color with the palette knife.

BRUSHWORK TECHNIQUES

The Brush

Can brushes be used to mix colors? Yes, but it involves more laborious cleaning than mixing with the palette knife. Therefore, it is advisable to have several brushes of various sizes in order to ease the burden of cleaning the same brush every time. Mixing colors with unwashed brushes containing paint residues will gradually affect and dirty your colors. In general, painters use the palette knife to place the paint in an area for mixing. Then they use the brush to mix the colors together and apply them directly on the canvas.

The type and size of the brushes used depend on the painter's style and personality.

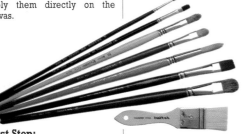

First Step: Preparing the Colors

A small brush is good for separating and mixing very tiny quantities of paint. A medium-size brush is more suitable for separating larger quantities of color (whether on the palette or the canvas).

The dirty brushes are easiest to clean while they are still wet. Place them in turpentine, then, with a piece of newspaper, remove the mass of paint. Finally, wash the brush with soap and hot water.

Second Step: Mixing the Paint

Follow the same operation as that used with the palette knife. By making circular movements with the brush and then sweeping it back and forth, you obtain a gradual blending of the two colors. With practice, you will be able to obtain very homogenous blends for subtle shades of color.

Mixing colors with a brush.

Third Step: Applying the Paint on the Canvas or Support

With a brush, it is common to blend together colors previously applied on the canvas while they are still wet.

Remember

• Always clean your implements thoroughly after each mix. Unclean brushes and palette knives dirty new color mixtures.
• It is essential to clean everything when you finish a painting session. l. This keeps implements in tiptop condition. 2. Color mixtures that are left to dry on the palette are difficult to clean, and they also make the painter's work more difficult when he tries to visualize the colors he needs for

Cleaning a brush by rubbing it in the palm of the hand with soap.

a new mixture, especially when he needs to prepare small quantities of color.
• Dried paint on the palette knife can be removed with the aid of a knife. As for brushes, there is a special cleaning product called "Brush Cleaner & Preservative." But as well as being laborious to use, it tends to gradually wear down the bristles of the brush.

A Special Technique

The artist's hands can also be used as painting implements. The fingertips, the side of the finger, and the palm can all be used to blend oil colors.

By moving the finger up and down or making circular movements, the painter can blend the colors directly on the canvas. This technique produces homogenous color blends and a satin-like finish, thus heightening the chiaroscuro.

Blending with a finger.

PAINTING WITH THREE COLORS AND WHITE

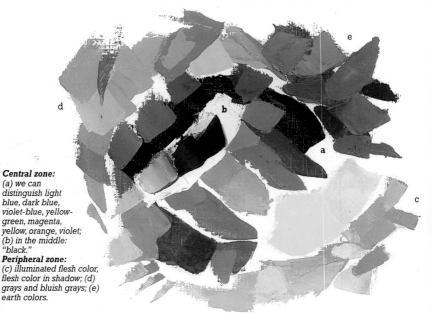

Central zone:
(a) we can distinguish light blue, dark blue, violet-blue, yellow-green, magenta, yellow, orange, violet; (b) in the middle: "black."
Peripheral zone:
(c) illuminated flesh color, flesh color in shadow; (d) grays and bluish grays; (e) earth colors.

The Primary Pigment Colors

All the colors reproduced on this page were obtained using Prussian blue, rose madder, cadmium yellow lemon, and white. These are the pigment colors that most closely resemble cyan blue, magenta, and yellow, and which are employed in graphic arts (where the colors are more balanced and the mixtures more accurate). Although there is a slight tonal difference, by adding white we can approximate our colors to the theoretical ones.

Patches

• **Central zone:** The colors in this area contain light blue, dark blue, violet-blue, green, blue-green, yellow-green, purple-red, red, yellow, orange, violet, and black. Let's now see how these colors were obtained.

1. By mixing the primary colors, cadmium yellow lemon, rose madder, and Prussian blue, together two at a time and in equal quantities, we obtain the three secondary colors: red, green, and dark blue.

2. By mixing the primary colors with secondary colors in pairs, we obtain the tertiary colors. Since there are three secondary colors and three primary colors, there are six tertiary colors in total: blue-green, violet, violet-blue, carmine, orange, and yellow-green.

3. By mixing the three primary colors together, we obtain black. This is the result of subtractive synthesis, in other words, mixing colors to take away light.

With the exception of black, the other colors in the very center were obtained by mixing two primary colors together.

• **Peripheral zone:** These are illuminated flesh colors: cadmium yellow lemon and rose madder with white.

Flesh color in shadow: created with the three primary colors and white.

Grays, bluish grays: also created with the three primary colors and white.

Remember

The primary colors are also used to produce flesh colors in shadow, grays, and earth tones. How is it possible to obtain such a wide range from the same colors? The answer lies in the fact that the proportions of each primary color you add to a mixture are different every time (see page 26).

SECONDARY PIGMENT COLORS

CYL + RM
↓
red

CYL + PB
↓
green

RM + PB
↓
dark blue

Mixing Two Pigment Primary Colors

By mixing in pairs the three primary pigment colors, cadmium yellow lemon, rose madder, and Prussian blue, we obtain the secondary pigment colors: green, red, and dark blue.

Secondaries: Green, Red, and Dark Blue

We will begin by using equal amounts of primary colors.

Secondary Red
With the aid of a palette knife, we scoop up two approximately equal amounts of the two primary colors, yellow and rose madder. The mixture of the two colors results in red, a secondary pigment color.

Secondary Green
Using a palette knife, we scoop up two approximately equal amounts of two primary colors, yellow and blue. The mixture produces green, a secondary pigment color.

Secondary Blue
With the aid of a palette knife, we prepare two approximately equal amounts of the two primary colors, rose madder and blue. The mixture creates dark blue, a secondary pigment color. (Blues are very dark, so it can be differentiated by adding a touch of white.)

Observation

On the difficulty of measuring quantities of paint: On page 19, we recommended using the palette knife as a measuring device. The obvious limitation is that this implement allows only rough measurements. But with practice you will quickly learn how to obtain the approximate proportions of each color.

TERTIARY COLORS

Mixing Primary and Secondary Colors

A tertiary color is obtained by mixing a primary color with a secondary color, which already contains that same primary color. So, only two primary colors are required to obtain a tertiary color. Likewise, each primary color can produce two tertiary colors. To create a tertiary color you require (approximately) equal parts of either color. Therefore each tertiary color needs two primary colors in 3-to-1 proportions.

CYL + PB
↓
green + CYL
↓
yellow-green

Tertiary: Yellow-Green

Yellow-green consists of more yellow than blue, so we need a greater quantity of the former. The yellow is then gradually added to the blue until the desired tone is obtained.

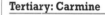

CYL + RM
↓
red + RM
↓
carmine

Tertiary: Carmine

Given that carmine requires more rose madder than yellow, we prepare a greater quantity of rose madder than yellow with the palette knife. The rose madder is then gradually added to the yellow until the desired tone is obtained.

RM + PB
↓
dark blue + PB
↓
violet-blue

Tertiary: Violet-Blue

Note: ultramarine blue is comparable to violet-blue.

Given that violet-blue requires more blue than rose madder, we prepare a greater quantity of Prussian blue than rose madder with the palette knife. The Prussian blue is then gradually added to the rose madder until the desired tone is obtained.

CYL + PB
↓
green + PB
↓
blue-green

Tertiary: Blue-Green

Note: emerald green is comparable to blue-green.

Given that blue-green is composed of more blue than yellow, we prepare a greater quantity of blue than yellow with the palette knife. The blue is then gradually added to the yellow until the desired tone is obtained.

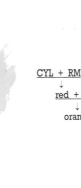

CYL + RM
↓
red + CYL
↓
orange

Tertiary: Orange

Because orange requires more yellow than rose madder, we prepare a greater quantity of yellow than rose madder with the palette knife. The yellow is then gradually added to the rose madder until the desired tone is obtained.

RM + PB
↓
dark blue + RM
↓
violet

Tertiary: Violet

Given that violet requires more rose madder than Prussian blue, we prepare a greater quantity of rose madder than blue with the palette knife. The rose madder is then gradually added to the Prussian blue until the desired tone is obtained.

COMPLEMENTARY COLORS

Theoretical Black

In theory, when we mix in equal parts a primary color with the secondary color (see page 9), that is, its complement, we obtain black. To put it another way, we must mix two parts of a primary color with one part of another primary color and one part of a third primary color. Note that the three samples of "black" are more akin to dirty colors than real black. On pages 54 and 55, you will find more in-depth information on how to create pure blacks and brilliant blacks using standard colors.

Other Dark Colors

Combinations of secondary and tertiary colors in equal parts mostly produce dark colors. When two primary colors are mixed together (this time in a 5-to-3 proportion), the range of greens, violets, and oranges are increased. However, other colors that are the result of mixtures of the three primary colors in unequal parts tend to gray according to the rules of subtractive synthesis. Only a small

(a) 2 parts rose madder, 1 part yellow, 1 part blue. (b) 2 parts cadmium yellow, 1 part rose madder, 1 part Prussian blue. (c) 2 parts Prussian blue, 1 part cadmium yellow lemon, 1 part rose madder. By adding a touch of white, we can bring out the real color of these mixtures.

proportion of colors in this group are defined as colors in their own right. These colors can be obtained from various theoretical proportions, but they are not of much help to the painter. It is best to adapt this theory to the artist's palette work. Consequently, proportions are expressed in terms of "plenty of," "considerably more of," or even "a lot of," "considerably less of," and "just a hint of."

Remember

Ochre is obtained by mixing plenty of yellow, less rose madder, and just a touch of blue. We can create sienna with similar quantities of yellow and rose madder, plus very little blue. Umber can be produced from a combination of plenty of rose

madder, much less yellow, and a little blue.

Conclusion: Earth colors, ochre, and umber are neutral colors, because they are colors that are the result of a mixture of two complementary colors in unequal proportions (see the definition of neutral colors on page 10).

Practicality: A Concrete Example

If we require a flesh color in shadow, the following primary colors plus a lot of white are required: cadmium yellow lemon and rose madder, and Prussian blue in less abundance. If we mix the three primary colors together, we risk darkening or "graying" the color. On the other hand, if we merely wish to darken a flesh color, all we need do is blend the three primary colors separately, then combine this mixture with the flesh color mixture so that their final proportions in the resulting color will be entirely different.

The Use of Manufactured Colors

It is often more convenient to use standard or commercially manufactured colors than to create your own from primary colors. The reason for this is that primary color mixtures have a tendency to gray due to a lack of "light" and contrast. Of course, it is possible to paint with the three primary colors and white, but the task is made more difficult. Nonetheless, it is well worth trying it out.

Samples of dark colors. Among others, we can identify ochre and several earth colors.

OTHER COLORS, OTHER INTERMEDIATE COLORS

A Choice: The Primary Colors

The three primary colors, cadmium yellow lemon, rose madder, and Prussian blue, best corroborate color theory (by means of subtractive synthesis). We can use them to obtain the cleanest mixtures, and the secondary and tertiary colors that

derive from them provide us with a reference for obtaining other mixtures with other colors.

Other Colors: Another Choice

Let's use cadmium yellow medium, cadmium red, and ultramarine blue as an example.

How to obtain intermediate colors:

SECONDARIES   TERTIARIES

1   2   3   4   5   6

green   blue-green   yellow-green

red   purple-red   orange

dark blue   violet-blue   violet

Columns 1, 3, and 5 are the results of mixtures obtained with primary colors, while columns 2, 4, and 6 are mixtures obtained with cadmium yellow medium, cadmium red, and ultramarine blue. The colors are mixed in equal parts to produce the secondary colors. And the primaries and secondaries are mixed in equal parts to produce the tertiary colors. The second choice mixtures are closely related to one another and are warmer than the mixtures obtained with the primary colors.

Observations

• A green can be obtained from a mixture of a group of yellows and a group of blues in the proportions the artist deems necessary; the chromatic characteristics of this green depend directly on the type of yellow and blue chosen.

• Standard greens (permanent green and emerald green) are intermediate colors in the chromatic wheel. They can be used to create a wide range of yellow-greens (when mixed with yellows) and blue-greens (when mixed with blues).

• Mixing a standard green (manufactured color) with another color means that the artist is in

reality adding yellow and blue to this color.

• Likewise, by mixing a color from a group of yellows with a color from a group of reds, in varying proportions, you get a wide range of oranges, yellows, and reds.

• A mixture created from a group of reds and a group of blues, varying the proportions, allows us to obtain violet colors ranging from the bluest to the reddest, whose chromatic characteristics depend on the red and blue colors chosen.

• It is convenient to classify standard colors into groups. Thus, violet is basically a tertiary color containing blue and abundant red. If you use this

color—a combination of red and blue—you will have to study its behavior when mixing it with other colors. Violet is useful for increasing the range of purple-violet-blue ranges.

• In all these examples, we have only mentioned two colors from their representative groups. For instance, green can be created with a mixture of yellow (which itself can be a mix of yellows) and blue (a mix of blues) and green can be added to it. The inclusion of a color from a third group, such as red (simple or mixed), compels the artist to enter the world of complementary and neutral colors, subjects that we will study more closely on pages 32 to 35, 40 to 41, 70 to 73, and 76 to 77.

CADMIUM YELLOW LEMON

Characteristics

Cadmium yellow lemon is the lightest of all the yellows. It is the primary yellow. As its name suggests, it has a cool lemony quality. It is an opaque color, and when mixed removes transparency. This yellow dries more slowly than other manufactured colors, a characteristic that can be easily observed, since it is the last color to dry on a painting. When mixed with white, cadmium yellow lemon does not display a significant gradation of tones.

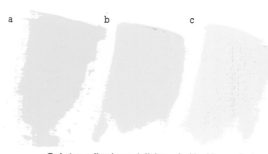

Cadmium yellow lemon is lightened with white, producing a limited gradation of tones.
a. intense color (only cadmium yellow lemon)
b. medium tone (incorporating white)
c. light tone (adding more white)

Examples

The result of combining cadmium yellow lemon in equal parts with each one of the other colors, classified from warm to cool. The examples reproduced on this page demonstrate its effect on various colors.

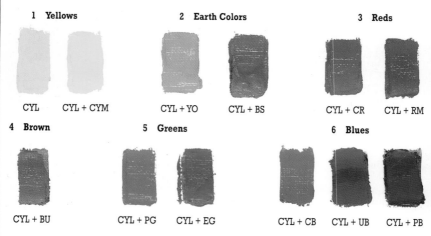

1 Yellows
CYL   CYL + CYM

2 Earth Colors
CYL + YO   CYL + BS

3 Reds
CYL + CR   CYL + RM

4 Brown
CYL + BU

5 Greens
CYL + PG   CYL + EG

6 Blues
CYL + CB   CYL + UB   CYL + PB

Specific Observations of the Range

Cadmium yellow lemon:
1. Reduces the orange hue of cadmium yellow medium.
2. Increases the range of ochres and earths with a greenish tendency.
3. Produces red of a cool tendency.
4. Mixed with burnt umber creates a markedly greenish tone.

5. Produces light, pure, brilliant, and cool greens.
6. Combined with blues produces a wide variety of green tones: with cobalt blue creates a lighter green and with Prussian blue produces a darker green.

COMPARISON WITH THE EXAMPLES OF:

- Cadmium yellow medium **p. 30**
- Yellow ochre **p. 32**

General Observations

• Cadmium yellow lemon lends all mixtures a cool hue with a greenish tendency, a direct result of its lemony quality. This is evident when comparing it to cadmium yellow medium.
• This color is used to produce yellows, ochres, reds, and greens.
• As the primary yellow, it is a main component of orange and carmine-red (tertiary colors).

A

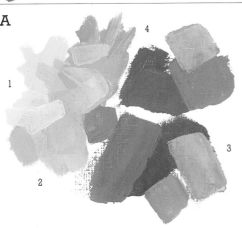

B

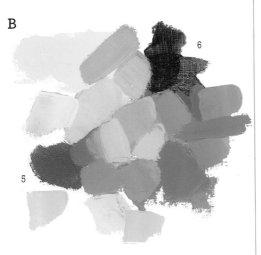

C

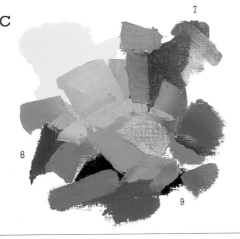

Ranges with Cadmium Yellow Lemon

The following ranges can be obtained by mixing cadmium yellow lemon with another color, varying the proportions, with or without white:

Yellow, Neutral, Orange, and Red Ranges

The **yellow range** is produced by combining yellows (1).

A limited **neutral range** can also be created with ochre (2).

Combined with red or rose madder, cadmium yellow lemon produces an **orange range**. They are luminous and bright colors, especially with rose madder. It is important to remember that you need plenty of yellow and little red to create orange (3).

To obtain the **red range**, you begin with a dark red, with abundant rose madder, and a little yellow, which should be gradually added to the mixture (4).

All the colors in group A (yellow, orange, red, neutral ochre) are warm.

Yellow-Green, Green, and Blue-Green Ranges

As you can see in group B, there is a noticeable difference between the mixtures obtained with one or another of the greens: permanent green (5) and emerald green (6). Mixtures produced with permanent green are slightly warmer. This color can be used to create a wide range of exquisite yellow-green colors.

Likewise, each blue can produce tones of different tendencies, as in group C: combined with cobalt blue we get dirtier greens, although somewhat less so than with ultramarine blue. The brightest green is obtained with Prussian blue. To create **yellow-greens** we have to add abundant yellow and very little blue (7). The **greens** are obtained through mixtures of approximately equal quantities of yellow and blue (8). The **blue-green** tones are the result of a mixture of abundant blue and little yellow (9).

The yellow-greens, greens, and blue-greens are cool. The blue-greens are cooler than the greens and, in turn, the greens are cooler than the yellows, in the same degree of saturation and luminosity.

The yellow-green range combined with cadmium yellow lemon has a markedly cool tendency.

MORE INFORMATION
- Secondary and tertiary colors **p. 23 to 25**

CADMIUM YELLOW MEDIUM

Characteristics

Cadmium yellow medium is one of the group of yellows. Compared with cadmium yellow lemon, this yellow is darker, with a tendency toward orange. It is an opaque color. Like all cadmium colors, it is permanent. Cadmium yellow medium can be lightened with cadmium yellow lemon and with white.

This type of yellow is the most appropriate for use as a dark yellow, when mixed with red.

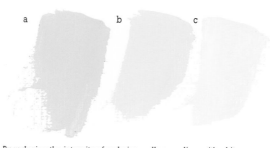

By reducing the intensity of cadmium yellow medium with white, you can see how the abundant white lightens the tone and the mixture becomes a creamy yellow.

a. intense color (only cadmium yellow medium)
b. medium tone (incorporating white)
c. light tone (adding more white)

Examples

The result of combining cadmium yellow medium in equal parts with each one of the other colors, classified from warm to cool. The examples reproduced on this page demonstrate its effect on various colors.

1 Yellows

CYM + CYL   CYM

2 Earth colors

CYM + YO   CYM + BS

3 Reds

CYM + CR   CYM + RM

4 Brown

CYM + BU

5 Greens

CYM + PG   CYM + EG

6 Blues

CYM + CB   CYM + UB   CYM + PB

Specific Observations of the Range

1. The tinting capacity of cadmium yellow medium is greater than that of cadmium yellow lemon.

2. The samples with ochre and sienna exhibit an orange tendency.

3. Cadmium yellow medium can be used for orange-red tone.

4. Combined with umber we get a mixture verging on green.

5. These yellow-greens are warm.

6. These greens are warm, verging on an olive tone. The brightest color is obtained with Prussian blue.

COMPARISON WITH THE RANGE OF:

• Cadmium yellow lemon **p. 28**
• Yellow ochre **p. 32**

General Observations

Cadmium yellow medium:
• Lends all mixtures a warm hue, an orange tendency, the result of its orange quality.
• Produces yellows, ochres, reds, and greens.
• Can form part of a mixture of orange and dark reds.
• Combined with ultramarine blue results in a grayish green.

A

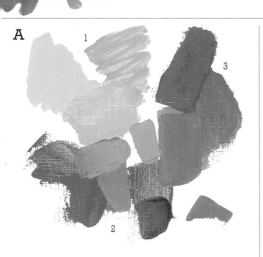

B

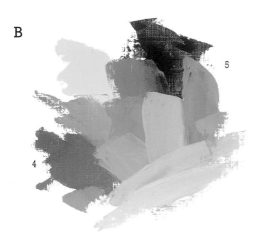

C

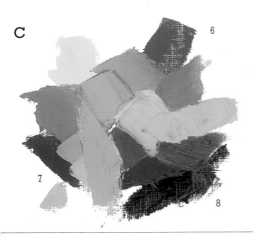

Ranges with Cadmium Yellow Medium

By mixing cadmium yellow medium with another color and varying the proportions, with or without white, we can obtain the following ranges:

Neutral, Orange, and Red Ranges

Neutral range (1). Combined with ochre with or without white, cadmium yellow medium increases the range of ochres and earth colors in the same way that cadmium yellow lemon did, although in this case a golden hue is produced.

Orange range (2). Obtained with a mixture of cadmium yellow lemon with cadmium red or rose madder with or without white. This blend requires plenty of yellow and little red for the orange. With cadmium yellow medium, the orange ranges become more reddish than with cadmium yellow lemon.

Red range (3). Cadmium yellow medium is combined with red and rose madder. Only a touch of yellow is needed to produce darker reds.

Yellows, oranges, ochres, and reds are warm colors (A).

Yellow-Green, Green, and Blue-Green Ranges

A mixture (B) of cadmium yellow medium with permanent green (4) and emerald green (5) with or without white. The greens are not as light as when mixed with cadmium yellow lemon. The greens take on a decidedly warm tendency, the direct result of the orange quality of cadmium yellow medium. The **yellow-greens** are warmer than those obtained with cadmium yellow lemon.

By mixing (C) cadmium yellow medium with cobalt blue (6), ultramarine blue (7), and Prussian blue (8), with or without white, we can see how each blue acquires different tendencies.

The greens are brighter with Prussian blue, and darker and dirtier with cobalt blue and ultramarine blue, but all have a warm tendency.

The **yellow-blues** (with abundant cadmium yellow medium), **greens** (with approximately equal parts of yellow and blue) are warmer than the colors produced with cadmium yellow lemon.

MORE INFORMATION

· Mixtures with cadmium yellow lemon **p. 29**

YELLOW OCHRE

Characteristics

Yellow ochre belongs to the group of yellows, but it is an earth color. This neutral color can be recomposed with plenty of yellow, a little rose madder, and just the slightest hint of blue. Yellow ochre is darker than cadmium yellow lemon and cadmium yellow medium, with a markedly golden tendency. It is a very opaque color. Note the intense color sample. Yellow ochre is permanent. It can be lightened with cadmium yellow lemon or cadmium yellow medium and white.

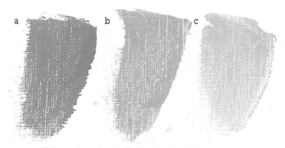

Yellow ochre mixed with abundant white becomes creamy:
a. intense color (only ochre)
b. medium tone (incorporating white)
c. light tone (adding more white)

Examples

The result of combining yellow ochre in equal parts with each one of the other colors, classified from warm to cool. The examples reproduced on this page demonstrate its effect on other colors.

1 Yellows
YO + CYL   YO + CYM

2 Earth Colors
YO   YO + BS

3 Reds
YO + CR   YO + RM

4 Brown
YO + BU

5 Greens
YO + PG   YO + EG

6 Blues
YO + CB   YO + UB   YO + PB

Specific Observations of the Range

1. Ochre darkens yellows, producing golden ochre colors.
2. It lightens sienna, producing a lighter burnt earth tone.
3. The reds are warm, but dirtier than with cadmium yellow lemon and cadmium yellow medium.
4. Ochre lightens umber and lends it a greenish tendency.

5. These are somber greens: very warm with permanent green, cooler with emerald green.
6. Combined with cobalt blue and ultramarine blue, the colors become very dirty. With Prussian blue, on the other hand, the green is dark but clean.

COMPARISON WITH THE RANGE OF:

- Cadmium yellow lemon **p. 28**
- Cadmium yellow medium **p. 30**

General Observations

- As a neutral color, yellow ochre tends to dirty colors. It is advisable to use it with care. Nonetheless this color can be used to harmonize the whole mixture.
- Yellow ochre produces ochres, earth colors, dull reds, warm greens, and somber greens when mixed with permanent green, emerald green, and Prussian blue.

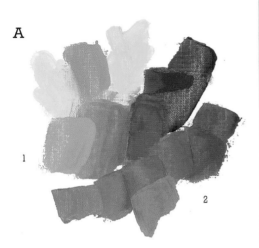

A

1

2

B

4

3

C

5

7

6

Ranges with Yellow Ochre

Mixing yellow ochre with another color, with or without white, produces neutral ranges.

Neutral Ranges

Ochre range (1). This is a wide range, obtained by mixing ochre with yellows, with or without white, and darkening with earth colors.

Earth range of a reddish tendency (2). Ochre with red and rose madder (especially with rose madder), with or without white. All earth colors, yellows, and reddish tones are neutral colors of a warm tendency (A).

Neutral green range (B). Obtained by mixing ochre with greens: permanent green (3) and emerald green (4). This is a highly harmonic range of neutral colors.

They become warm neutral colors when the proportion of ochre is greater than that of green. When the proportion of green in the mixture is greater than the amount of ochre, neutral colors of a cool tendency are produced.

Brown, gray, greenish, bluish-green color ranges (C). They are obtained with mixtures of yellow ochre with each blue, with or without white. Note the differences with each blue: mixtures with cobalt blue (5), with ultramarine blue (6), and with Prussian blue (7). Pay close attention to the subtleties of the hues, the harmony of the whole.

Browns, grays, bluish greens, and so forth, are all neutral colors of a warm tendency when there is more ochre than blue, and neutral colors of a cool tendency when there is more blue.

White

The inclusion of white in mixtures creates a wide tonal range. Its effect on the mixtures modifies the temperature, cooling down the warm tendencies, and warming up the cool tendencies. This is an additional technique for harmonizing neutral colors.

MORE INFORMATION
· Mixtures with ochre **p. 63**
· Mixtures of yellow with green **p. 65**
· Neutral harmonic range 1 **p. 70**
· Neutral harmonic range 2 **p. 72**

BURNT SIENNA

Characteristics

Burnt sienna is a red earth color. It is classified as a neutral color due to its composition of cadmium yellow lemon and rose madder in almost equal parts and very little Prussian blue. This color can also be obtained by mixing abundant rose madder, less ochre, and only the slightest hint of Prussian blue. When mixed with other colors, it brings out its yellow, rose madder, or blue part; therefore, the mixtures will also be neutral. Burnt sienna is a very transparent color that tends to blacken, for which reason it should be used sparingly and almost never on its own, always in a mixture. It can be lightened with yellows, ochre, and white.

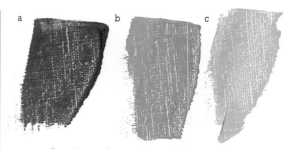

Burnt sienna takes on a characteristic salmon color when white is added to it:
a. intense color (only burnt sienna)
b. medium tone (incorporating white)
c. light tone (adding more white)

Examples

The result of combining burnt sienna in equal parts with each one of the other colors, classi-fied from warm to cool. The examples reproduced on this page demonstrate its effect on various colors.

1 **Yellows**

BS + CYL   BS+ CYM

2 **Earth Colors**

BS + YO   BS

3 **Reds**

BS + CR   BS + RM

4 **Brown**

BS + BU

5 **Greens**

BS +PG   BS + EG

6 **Blues**

BS + CB   BS + UB   BS + PB

Specific Observations of the Range

Burnt sienna:
1. and 2. Produces a range of darker ochres of a copper-colored tendency, more reddish and earthy.
3. Darkens reds, to a much greater extent than rose madder. It tends toward a brown red.
4. When mixed with umber, creates a dark color. The tinting capacity of umber is greater than sienna.

5. Combined with greens pro-duces very dark colors, emerald green being the darkest.
6. With blues gives rise to very dark colors.

General Observations

• Burnt sienna lends its com-ponents—yellow and red in equal parts and a small amount of blue—to any color mix. Sienna darkens colors with an earthy hue. Mixing it with other colors in different proportions is recommended.

• It produces dark, earthy, and reddish earth colors.
• Burnt sienna must be mixed with great care, especially with greens and blues. By using the appropriate proportions you can obtain many neutral colors.

COMPARISON WITH THE RANGE OF:

• Burnt umber **p. 40**

A

1

2

3

B

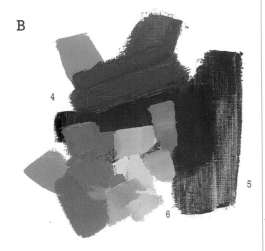

4

5

6

C

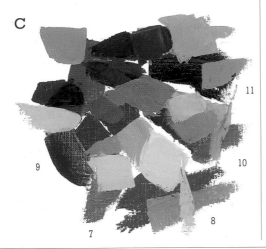

11

9

10

8

7

Ranges with Burnt Sienna

By mixing burnt sienna with another color and varying the proportions, with or without white, we obtain neutral ranges.

Ranges with Earth, Reddish Ochre, Reddish Earth

A combination of burnt sienna with yellows and ochres, with or without white, produces a perfect harmony of colors (1).

Mixing sienna and ochre (a little yellow and a little red) increases the range of earth tones, which are produced very cleanly even when white is added (2).

Burnt sienna with cadmium yellow or rose madder (with or without white) (3) increases the range of reddish earth colors which harmonize with (1) and (2).

One interesting experiment is to make your own burnt sienna, using abundant rose madder, slightly less ochre, and very little Prussian blue (4).

This example is a standard commercially manufactured burnt sienna (5). Compare (4) to (5). Our color is very similar to the standard color, except that it is less clean and less transparent: note the degree of transparency of the commercial product.

This flesh color has been created with ochre, burnt sienna, yellow, and red (6).

All the colors included in groups A and B are warm neutral colors.

Ranges with Brown, Grays, Bluish Gray

Mixing burnt sienna with emerald green, or with Prussian blue in equal parts, with white results in grays. The burnt sienna takes on the role of a red. Let's take a closer look at group C:

Burnt sienna with permanent green produces browns (7). With cobalt blue we get more brown tones (8). This is burnt sienna with emerald green (9). Here we have the same color, this time with ultramarine blue (10). And here with Prussian blue (11). The results of colors (9), (10), and (11) are very dark colors obtained from mixtures of equal parts. But a combination of burnt sienna with each green and each blue, in different proportions with or without white produces many neutral ranges with the obvious influence of the predominant color.

All the browns, grays, bluish grays, and so forth are neutral colors.

| **MORE INFORMATION** |
- Neutral harmonic range 1 **p. 70**
- Neutral harmonic range 2 **p. 72**

CADMIUM RED

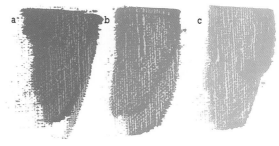

Characteristics

Cadmium red belongs to the group of red colors. We could define it as a "red red." It is semi-transparent and, like all cadmium colors, is permanent. It can be lightened with yellow and white.

Cadmium red is the most suitable color for obtaining a light red.

It can be turned into pink by reducing the saturation of the red cadmium with white (which is very characteristic of this color).

When the intensity of cadmium red is reduced with white it tends toward a very pure pink:
a. intense color (only cadmium red)
b. medium tone (incorporating white)
c. light tone (adding more white)

Examples

The result of combining cadmium red in equal parts with each one of the other colors, classified from warm to cool. The examples reproduced on this page demonstrate its effect on various colors.

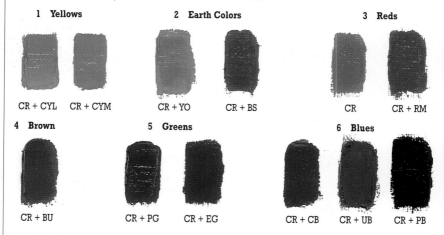

1 Yellows   CR + CYL   CR + CYM

2 Earth Colors   CR + YO   CR + BS

3 Reds   CR   CR + RM

4 Brown   CR + BU

5 Greens   CR + PG   CR + EG

6 Blues   CR + CB   CR + UB   CR + PB

Specific Observations of the Range

Cadmium red mixed with:
1. Yellows results in oranges.
2. Earth, ochre, and sienna produces brown colors.
3. Rose madder creates an intense deep red.
4. Umber gives rise to a reddish, burnt, very interesting earth color.
5. Permanent green tends toward brown, and with emerald green verges on "black."
6. Cobalt blue produces a magnificent burnt color; with ultramarine blue it is more metallic, and with Prussian blue it is almost black.

General Observations

• There is a general reddish tendency in the example colors that disappears only with emerald green and especially Prussian blue (also with ultramarine blue, but to a lesser extent). Mixed with Prussian blue, cadmium red deserves special attention.

• Cadmium red can be used to create oranges, reds, earth colors, and browns.

• Red is the complement of emerald green, but it is also advisable to pay special attention to the proportions of mixtures with permanent greens and blues.

COMPARISON WITH THE RANGE OF:

• Burnt sienna p. 34
• Rose madder p. 38

A

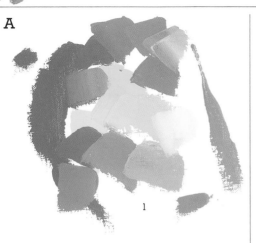

1

B

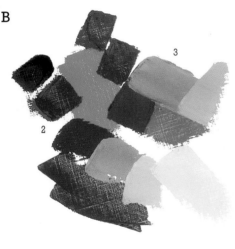

3

2

C

6

5

4

Ranges with Cadmium Red

Combining cadmium red with another color, in varying proportions, with or without white, produces some very interesting ranges:

Neutral, Orange, and Red Ranges

The orange range (1). Obtained by mixing cadmium red with yellows, this requires more yellow than cadmium red (like a tertiary color) with or without white. This range is very luminous and clean.

Neutral ranges with earth. Combined with earth colors, whether ochre or sienna (see page 63), cadmium red produces a splendid harmonized range.

Red range. Cadmium red with rose madder gives way to intense deep red colors; see (2), page 39.

All these colors are warm and therefore harmonize with one another.

Green Ranges

Neutral range with greens. Cadmium red is a complementary color of emerald green (2), as well as with permanent green, but to a lesser degree (3).

With greens, cadmium red provides a wide range of grays, with mixtures in equal parts and white. In order to obtain interesting neutral reddish, burnt earth colors, it is essential to add more cadmium red to the mixtures.

Blue Ranges

How does cadmium red behave when combined with blue colors? Let's compare the results:

With cobalt blue (4).

With ultramarine blue (5).

With Prussian blue (6).

On page 27 you can see how cadmium red is used to make tertiary colors warmer than those produced with rose madder. They are somewhat dirtier mixtures, even though neutral colors are always dirty or grayish. It is worth noting the "solidness" of the intense versions of red and blue and the reduction of that solidness and contrast with lighter tones.

MORE INFORMATION
· Burnt sienna earth ranges **p. 35**
· Rose madder ranges **p. 39**

ROSE MADDER

Characteristics

Rose madder is a red color, one of the primary colors. It is the darkest red of the palette, with a markedly magenta tendency. This color is very transparent and permanent. It can be lightened with yellows, cadmium red, and white. Rose madder is the most suitable color for use as a dark red.

When blended with abundant white, rose madder produces a characteristic rose tone.

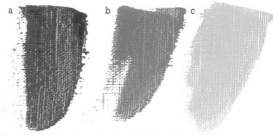

The color persists when white is added. The light tone is a luminous pink of a rose tendency.
a. intense color (only rose madder)
b. medium tone (incorporating white)
c. light tone (adding more white)

Examples

The result of combining rose madder in equal parts with each one of the other colors, classified from warm to cool. The samples reproduced on this page demonstrate its effect on various colors.

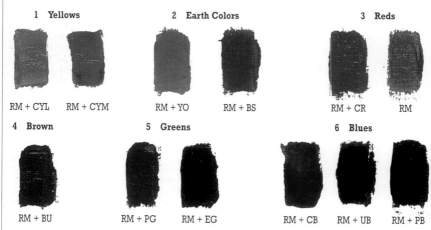

1 Yellows		2 Earth Colors		3 Reds	
RM + CYL	RM + CYM	RM + YO	RM + BS	RM + CR	RM

4 Brown	5 Greens		6 Blues		
RM + BU	RM + PG	RM + EG	RM + CB	RM + UB	RM + PB

Specific Observations of the Range

Rose madder combined with:
1. Yellows produces reds; the more orange-toned ones are the result of a mixture with cadmium yellow medium.
2. Ochre produces a reddish earth tone; mixed with burnt sienna it becomes a red-toned earth color.
3. Cadmium red produces an intense red.
4. Burnt umber produces a very dark mixture.

5. Green creates very dark colors, due to its being a complementary color. (This is the case even more with emerald green.)
6. Blues produces very dark colors, especially with Prussian blue.

General Observations

• Mixtures with rose madder produce oranges, dark reds, and reddish earth colors.
• Rose madder is also useful for obtaining "blacks" with burnt umber, emerald green, and Prussian blue. You can create dark colors when you mix it with permanent green, cobalt blue, and ultramarine blue.
• Note the color harmony in the first row of colors, all of which are warm.
• As a primary color, rose madder is used to obtain secondary and tertiary colors.

COMPARISON WITH THE RANGE OF:

• Cadmium red **p. 36**

A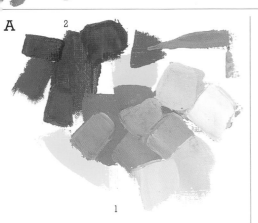

B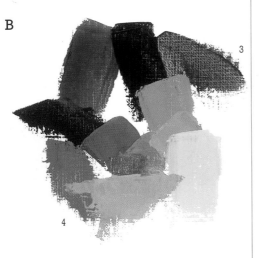

C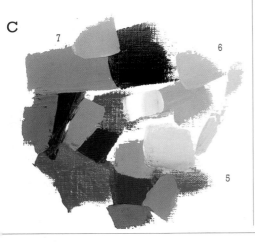

Ranges with Rose Madder

Blending rose madder with another color, in varied proportions, with or without white, we obtain the following interesting ranges:

Orange range (1). The result of a combination of rose madder with yellow. Considerably more yellow than rose madder is needed to obtain this range. They are warm colors.

Neutral earth range. Observe the examples. Mixed with ochre, rose madder produces luminous earth colors, while with sienna it produces reddish earth colors. See page 63. These are high quality neutral colors of a warm tendency.

Dark red range (2). With cadmium red, rose madder produces intense dark red colors, which are potent and very warm. These colors harmonize easily with those in the orange range (1).

The mixture of rose madder with green results in a magnificent **range of grays (B).**

This is the result of a mixture of rose madder and its complementary color emerald green (3).

More grays are obtained with permanent green (4).

Note the hardness of the intense colors and the subtle harmony of the whole due to the effect of adding white. There is a predominance of rose madder or green.

The mixtures in unequal proportions of rose madder with green, which in turn is composed of yellow and blue, are neutral colors (due to the use of the three primary colors).

Violet and purple ranges. These colors are obtained by mixing rose madder with each one of the blues, with or without white. (Remember that to obtain a violet we require more rose madder than blue, and in the case of purple, even more rose madder is needed.)

Note the mixtures with cobalt blue (5).

With ultramarine blue the tendency is less warm (6).

With Prussian blue, the colors are even cooler (7).

But all these colors appear to be purer than those produced from a mix with cadmium red.

These colors are cooler if they are of a bluish tendency, and warmer if the tendency is reddish.

MORE INFORMATION
· Burnt sienna **p. 35**
· Cadmium red **p. 37**

BURNT UMBER

Characteristics

Burnt umber is an earth color. One of the darkest earth colors, it belongs to the group of browns. It is classified as a neutral color because it consists of abundant carmine, much less yellow, and a touch of blue. Burnt umber is regarded as the coolest warm color. It is lightened by adding yellows, ochre, red, and white. Burnt umber is a very transparent color.

On the other hand, this color tends to blacken, so it should be used sparingly.

Another factor to bear in mind is its fast-drying quality; also, it is not advisable to apply it in thick layers.

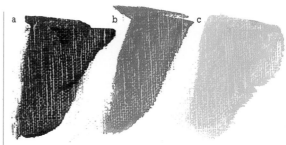

Burnt umber with white takes on a color between a burnt and creamy type of umber:
  a. intense color (only burnt umber)
  b. medium tone (incorporating white)
  c. light tone (adding more white)

Examples

The result of combining burnt umber in equal parts with each one of the other colors, classified from warm to cool. The samples reproduced on this page demonstrate its effect on various colors.

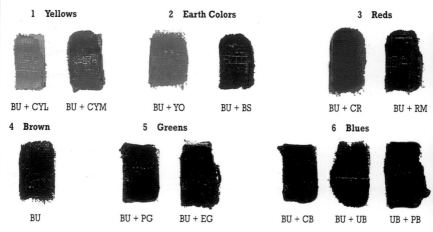

1 Yellows		2 Earth Colors		3 Reds	
BU + CYL	BU + CYM	BU + YO	BU + BS	BU + CR	BU + RM

4 Brown	5 Greens		6 Blues		
BU	BU + PG	BU + EG	BU + CB	BU + UB	UB + PB

Specific Observations of the Range

Burnt umber:
1. Mixed with yellows produces greenish colors.
2. Darkens ochre and increases the burnt appearance of burnt sienna.
3. Mixed with cadmium red produces an exquisite chocolate-colored reddish earth tone; mixed with rose madder it produces a very dark color.

5. Together with green creates very dark colors, the darkest obtained with emerald green.
6. Mixed with blues creates very dark colors. These samples are almost black, and the most intense of these blue blacks is obtained with Prussian blue.

COMPARISON WITH THE RANGE OF:
• Burnt sienna **p. 34**

General Observations

• Burnt umber can be used to obtain greenish ochre colors.
• It can also produce dark earth and burnt tones.
• Combined with rose madder, emerald green, and blue, burnt umber provides the foundation of black.
• As its name indicates, this color darkens significantly. Therefore, it should be used in small quantities.

A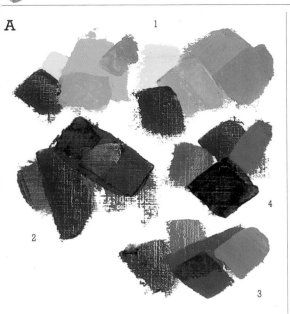

B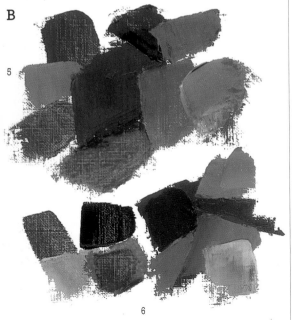

Ranges with Burnt Umber

Mixing burnt umber with another color, in varying proportions, with or without white, we can obtain the following ranges:

Neutral Ranges

From a combination of ochre and yellow, we can produce ochre colors of a greenish tendency, and greenish colors (1).

From a burnt umber mixture, countless shades of color can be achieved (2). Note the highly harmonious quality of this group.

With red (3) and with rose madder (4), we can obtain the most exquisite "chocolate" earth colors.

The color mixtures in (A) are neutral warm colors.

Here (B) we mix the burnt umber with two more colors at the same time:

A combination of burnt umber, emerald green and rose madder (with white) produces a wide range of grays (5). The predominant color of the mixture is always the most prominent thus, "gray gray," "gray brown," "madder gray."

Mixing burnt umber with rose madder and Prussian blue, in addition to white, results in a wide range of grays of varying tendencies.

Even with very dark colors there exists a notable harmony in the group of neutral colors (6).

Important. Burnt umber is an indispensable color for the painter, so it is important to know how to use it properly. It is a color with a remarkable tinting capacity, so it should be used sparingly in mixtures. Used in the correct manner, the artist can tone and reduce contrasts. Excessive usage of this burnt umber leads to very dirty colors.

MORE INFORMATION

• Burnt sienna **p. 35**

PERMANENT GREEN

Characteristics

Permanent green forms parts of the group of green colors. It derives from a combination of chrome oxide and cadmium yellow lemon. We could describe it as a light and luminous green that has a less bluish tendency than emerald green (see page 44). Permanent green is a semi-opaque color and, as its name suggests, is permanent. This green can be lightened with yellows, ochre, and white. When white is added to it, permanent green becomes a pastel green.

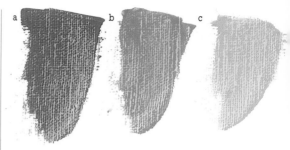

Permanent green mixed with white becomes a subtle but vibrant pastel green:

   a. intense color (only permanent green)
   b. medium tone (incorporating white)
   c. light tone (adding more white)

Examples

The result of combining permanent green in equal parts with each one of the other colors, classified from warm to cool. The samples reproduced on this page demonstrate its effect on various colors.

1 Yellows

PG + CYL   PG + CYM

2 Earth Colors

PG + YO   PG + BS

3 Reds

PG + CR   PG + RM

4 Brown

PG + BU

5 Greens

PG   PG + EM

6 Blues

PG + CB   PG + UB   PG + PB

Specific Observations of the Range

1. Cadmium yellow lemon lightens permanent green, lending it a cooler tendency than when mixed with cadmium yellow medium.

2. Combined with ochre, permanent green becomes olive green, and with sienna, a very burnt earth color.

3. By mixing rose madder with green we obtain a very dark color that indicates a degree of complementariness.

4. Permanent green mixed with burnt umber gives way to a very dark greenish color.

5. We can compare the hues of the two greens here.

6. With cobalt blue and ultramarine blue we obtain blue-greens, and with Prussian blue we obtain a very dark green.

COMPARISON WITH THE RANGE OF:

• Emerald green p. 44

General Observations

• Due to its warm tendency, permanent green can be used to obtain warm yellow-greens with the addition of yellow.

• It can obtain greens of an olive green tendency with ochre.

• All the mixtures of permanent green with reddish earth tones and browns produce even more burnt earth colors.

• Permanent green and rose madder can be combined to create dark colors.

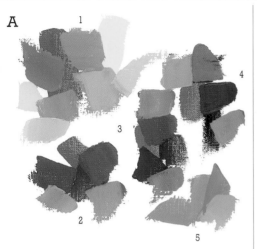

A

1

4

3

2

5

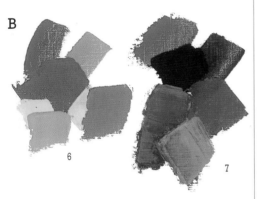

B

6

7

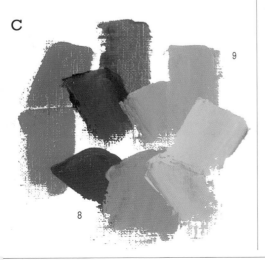

C

9

8

Ranges with Permanent Green

By mixing permanent green with another color, in varying proportions, with or without white, we can obtain the following neutral ranges:

Green Ranges

Yellow-greens obtained from mixtures of permanent green with cadmium yellow lemon result in cooler colors; mixtures with cadmium yellow medium are warmer (1).

Let's examine the greens and blue-greens obtained from a mix of permanent green with each blue:

With cobalt blue (2), with ultramarine blue (3), and with Prussian blue (4).

A wide range of blue-green colors is produced. There are notable differences in the mixtures with each blue.

If we add yellow to these blue-greens, we obtain a diversity of hues (5). And by adding yellow to the greens we can get an almost infinite number of yellow-green colors.

Note the pleasant chromatic harmony of group A.

> **MORE INFORMATION**
>
> • Emerald green **p. 45**
> • Yellow-greens **p. 68**

Neutral Ranges

Mixing permanent green with ochre and lightening it with cadmium yellow lemon and cadmium yellow medium plus white produces a range of olive green tones (6).

Made by combining permanent green and burnt sienna, the resultant earth color is very dark (7), but interesting, when suitably grayed with white. This range can also be enhanced by the addition of ochre colors.

Let's look at the mixtures obtained with the reddest colors of the palette (C):

A mixture of permanent green and cadmium red (8).

Also a combination of green and rose madder with or without white (9).

These are neutral colors, grays, and browns, whose tendencies depend on the predominant color of the mixture.

It is essential to pause for a moment and study the harmony of the neutral colors in groups B and C.

EMERALD GREEN

Characteristics

Emerald green could be classified as a tertiary color. It is a green with a bluish tendency. Compared with permanent green, this is a cool and a very transparent green. Nonetheless it is very permanent. You can lighten emerald green with various colors: yellows, ochre, and white.

When abundant white is added to emerald green, we obtain a bluish green.

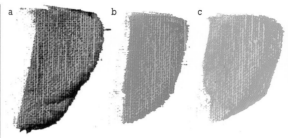

When emerald green is lightened with white, it acquires a bluish tendency.
a. intense color (only emerald green)
b. medium tone (incorporating white)
c. light tone (adding more white)

Examples

The result of combining emerald green in equal parts with each one of the other colors, classified from warm to cool. The examples reproduced on this page demonstrate its effect on various colors.

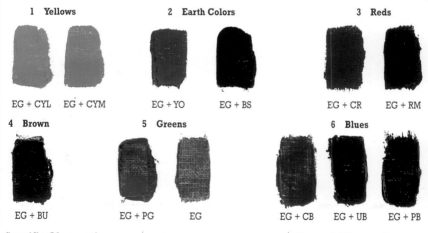

1 **Yellows**   EG + CYL   EG + CYM

2 **Earth Colors**   EG + YO   EG + BS

3 **Reds**   EG + CR   EG + RM

4 **Brown**   EG + BU

5 **Greens**   EG + PG   EG

6 **Blues**   EG + CB   EG + UB   EG + PB

Specific Observations of the Range

1. Emerald green can be pure and cool mixed with cadmium yellow lemon, and warmer mixed with cadmium yellow medium.

2. With ochre an olive green can be produced, and a very dark green with burnt sienna.

3. Emerald green can be used to darken reds. With red it produces a dark earth color; with rose madder the color is practically black.

4. Emerald green and burnt umber can be combined to create this dark color.

5. Mixed together, permanent and emerald green complement each other, giving way to a neutral green.

6. It is worth remembering that a combination of emerald green and cobalt blue produce an extraordinary blue-green. With respect to other mixtures, ultramarine blue blended with emerald green is darker, and even more so with Prussian blue.

General Observations

• Emerald green produces cooler greens than permanent green.

• It can also be used to obtain browns.

• With rose madder, burnt umber, and Prussian blue we can obtain a magnificent black.

COMPARISON WITH THE RANGE OF:

• Permanent green **p. 42**

Ranges with Emerald Green

Mixing emerald green with another color, with or without white and in varying proportions, we obtain the following ranges:

Green Ranges

By combining emerald green with cadmium yellow lemon or cadmium yellow medium, with or without white, we can obtain a whole range of greens (1). Greens are cooler with cadmium yellow lemon and warmer with cadmium yellow medium.

Deeper blue-greens can be produced by blending emerald green with cobalt blue (2), or with ultramarine blue (3), or with Prussian blue (4), with or without white. These three colors provide the painter with three types of blue-green colors.

Blue-greens lightened with yellow allow countless possibilities with greens and yellow-greens (5).

Yellow-greens are warmer colors, while greens and blue-greens are cooler (A).

Neutral Colors

With Earth Tones (B)

If we combine emerald green with ochres and yellows, we obtain a range of olive greens by adding white (6).

Mixing emerald green with burnt sienna produces grays and browns (7). Sienna is a color composed of red, so it is appropriate to mix it with green in very unequal proportions. By playing with ochre, the greenish tendency becomes darker than in the olive greens (6).

With Reds (C)

Since emerald green and rose madder are complementary colors, by mixing them together and adding white, we can obtain grays and neutral colors that bring out the predominant complementary color (8) (see page 72).

Emerald green and cadmium red are less complementary, although they both produce magnificent gray and neutral colors that, as mentioned earlier, reflect the most predominant color of the two (9).

Note the harmony of these neutral colors.

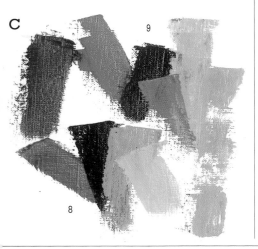

MORE INFORMATION

• Permanent green ranges **p. 43**

COBALT BLUE

Characteristics

Cobalt blue is a "blue blue," a neutral blue. It has a cooler tendency than ultramarine blue and a warmer tendency than Prussian blue. It is a semi-opaque color and is permanent. The lightest version of cobalt blue is obtained with a hint of cadmium yellow lemon (and we *mean* no more than a hint) and a lot of white. This is the lightest possible blue of the spectrum. By mixing cobalt blue with plenty of white you get a luminous blue.

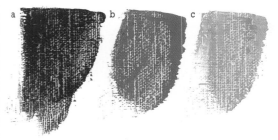

Notice how cobalt blue remains luminous after adding white.
a. intense color (only cobalt blue)
b. medium tone (incorporating white)
c. light tone (adding more white)

Examples

The result of combining cobalt blue in equal parts with each one of the other colors, classified from warm to cool. The examples reproduced on this page demonstrate its effect on various colors.

1 **Yellows**
CB + CYL   CB + CYM

2 **Earth Colors**
CB + YO   CB + BS

3 **Reds**
CB + CR   CB + RM

4 **Brown**
CB + BU

5 **Greens**
CB + PG   CB + EG

6 **Blues**
CB   CB + UB   CB + PB

Specific Observations of the Range

1. The light green produced by mixing cobalt blue with cadmium yellow lemon is cooler than the mixture containing cadmium yellow medium.
2. An olive green color can be obtained by blending cobalt blue with ochre, and a reddish brown is produced by blending it with burnt sienna.
3. Cobalt blue darkens the reds, and the darkest of them is produced with rose madder.
4. Cobalt blue and umber create a very dark color.
5. This very pure blue-green is obtained with emerald green.
6. Cobalt blue lightens other blues. The proportions for these mixtures reveal that the tinting capacity of cobalt blue is less than that of the other blues.

COMPARISON WITH THE RANGE OF:
• Ultramarine blue **p. 48**
• Prussian blue **p. 50**

General Observations

• Cobalt blue produces greens (yellow-greens, greens, and blue-greens).
• Ochre also creates greens, in this case olive greens. Sienna and umber mixed with cobalt blue produce several very interesting wine and earth colors.
• Due to its light and luminous tones, this neutral blue is ideal for use in any type of luminous shadow (See "How do you paint the color of shadows?" page 13).

Ranges with Cobalt Blue

Combining cobalt blue with another color, with or without white, and modifying the proportions, we obtain the following ranges:

Green and Blue-Green Ranges

Greens. Blended with cadmium yellow lemon, cobalt blue produces light greens; mixed with cadmium yellow medium, it produces duller and warmer greens (1).

Blue-green. Cobalt blue combined with permanent green (2), or with emerald green (3), with or without white, produces an interesting and wide range of cool colors.

Neutral Colors

Cobalt blue mixed with ochre and white gives way to very harmonized bluish grays and greenish grays (4).

Cobalt blue combined with burnt sienna and white produces brown and gray colors that display the greatest subtlety (see page 73).

These are neutral colors.

Cobalt Blue with Reds

Note the example with rose madder (B).

Mixing cobalt blue with rose madder with or without white opens up a wide range of possibilities. We get a range that extends from violet-blue to violet, mauve, and purple. Here we see three swatches:

A violet-blue tendency (5), a mauve-violet tendency (6), and a dull purple obtained by darkening the rose madder with a little cobalt blue (7). Note the general harmony of groups 5 and 6, and of 6 and 7.

In equal intensity, the color mixtures with blue are cooler in this group. As the proportion of rose madder increases, they become warmer.

A

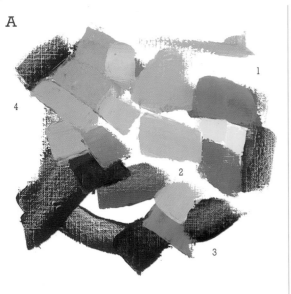

B

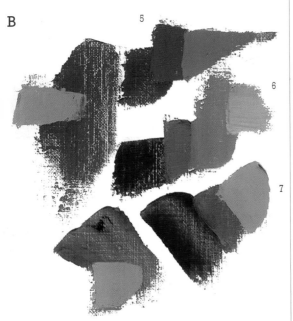

MORE INFORMATION

• Cobalt blue p. 37

ULTRAMARINE BLUE

Characteristics

Ultramarine blue belongs to the blue group. It is a violety blue with an obvious red tendency. This color is transparent and permanent.

Ultramarine blue's violet tendency makes it ideal for use as a dark blue in daylight conditions.

Combined with abundant white, we can obtain a warmer, more reddish type of blue.

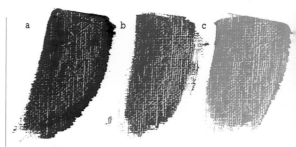

Combined with white, ultramarine blue maintains its reddish warm tendency.
a. intense color (only ultramarine blue)
b. medium tone (incorporating white)
c. light tone (adding more white)

Examples

The result of combining ultramarine blue in equal parts with each one of the other colors, classified from warm to cool. The samples reproduced on this page demonstrate its effect on various colors.

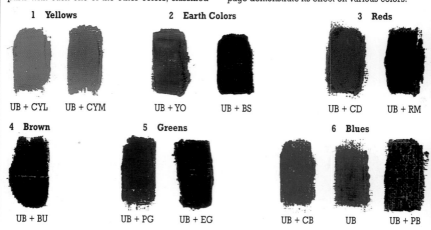

1 **Yellows**

UB + CYL   UB + CYM

2 **Earth Colors**

UB + YO   UB + BS

3 **Reds**

UB + CD   UB + RM

4 **Brown**

UB + BU

5 **Greens**

UB + PG   UB + EG

6 **Blues**

UB + CB   UB   UB + PB

Specific Observations of the Range

1. Mixed with cadmium yellow lemon, ultramarine blue produces this cool bluish green, while a warmer version is produced with cadmium yellow medium.

2. The results of these mixtures are dark greens.

3. With cadmium red, ultramarine blue produces a burnt tone, while with rose madder, it results in this very dark tone.

4. Umber with ultramarine blue produces a very dark color.

5. The combination of ultramarine blue with greens results in magnificent greenish blues.

6. These samples show how the blues can be increased by neutralizing the tendencies.

General Observations

Ultramarine blue:
• Produces greens, blue-greens, very dark greens, and browns.
• Produces violet colors when combined with red in unequal parts (see tertiary colors).

• With burnt sienna and umber produces very dark colors; it is best to treat them as neutral colors.

• Is best used for painting the color of less luminous shadows (see "How do you paint the color of shadows?" page 13), because its reddish tendency darkens the mixtures with other colors.

COMPARISON WITH THE RANGE OF:

• Cobalt blue p. 46
• Prussian blue p. 50

A

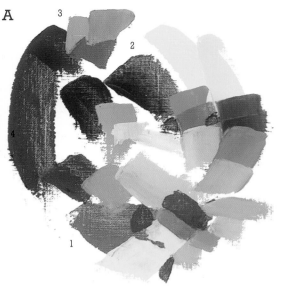

Ranges with Ultramarine Blue

By mixing ultramarine blue with another color, in varying proportions, with or without white, we obtain the following ranges:

Green Range

Ultramarine blue with yellow, with or without white (see pages 29 and 31).

Blue-Green Range

Ultramarine blue with permanent green, with or without white (1).

Combined with emerald green, the blue-greens are cooler (2).

These are cool colors. The ones that are more saturated and that contain more blue are the coolest.

Neutral Range

Ultramarine blue combined with ochre, with or without white, produces a range of greenish, grayish neutral colors (3).

Violet-Blue, Violet, and Mauve Ranges

Example (B): mixing ultramarine blue with rose madder.
• When blue predominates, we obtain violet-blue (4).
• If you are aiming for the proportions required for a tertiary color you get violet (5).
• These examples (6) have been produced with an evident predominance of rose madder. The result is a number of mauve tones.

These colors were obtained with a predominant amount of rose madder. By increasing the proportion of blue, the mixtures become cooler, while the tone remains the same.

B

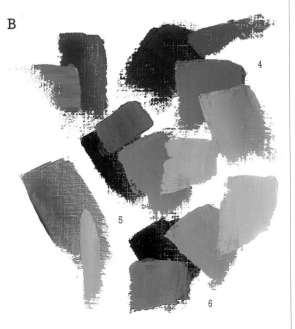

MORE INFORMATION

• Blue-green range **p. 47**
• Blue-green range **p. 51**
• Cadmium red range **p. 37**

PRUSSIAN BLUE

Characteristics

Prussian blue is a primary color. It is a blue of a coolish tendency, with a slight greenish tinge. This color is transparent but is not very permanent, so it tends to fade. It has a good tinting capacity, therefore it should be used sparingly. Prussian blue with abundant white produces a pastel blue color that is characteristic of its greenish tendency.

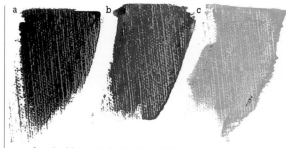

Prussian blue maintains its color well when blended with white.
a. intense color (only Prussian blue)
b. medium tone (incorporating white)
c. light tone (adding more white)

Examples

The result of combining Prussian blue in equal parts with each one of the other colors, classified from warm to cool. The samples reproduced on this page demonstrate its effect on various colors.

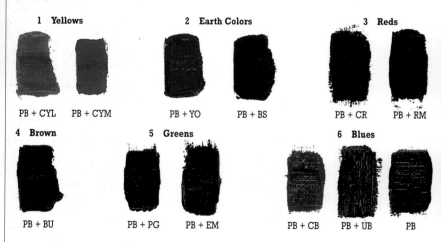

1 Yellows

PB + CYL   PB + CYM

2 Earth Colors

PB + YO   PB + BS

3 Reds

PB + CR   PB + RM

4 Brown

PB + BU

5 Greens

PB + PG   PB + EM

6 Blues

PB + CB   PB + UB   PB

Specific Observations of the Range

1. Combined with yellows, Prussian blue produces pure dark greens.

2. With ochre, it produces a dark green, and with burnt sienna, a very dark color.

3 and 4. These are dark brown colors; Prussian blue combined with umber is very dark.

5. These blue-greens are interesting, since they are clean and intense.

6. Mixing blues together allows the artist to increase the range of blues. Cobalt blue acts as a neutralizing element, while ultramarine blue produces a violet tendency. This range of tones and hues can only be achieved if Prussian blue is used in the smallest possible proportion as compared to that of the other blues. Example 6 does not demonstrate these small amounts.

COMPARISON WITH THE RANGE OF:

• Cobalt blue **p. 46**
• Ultramarine blue **p. 48**

General Observations

• The colors here are generally very dark.

• Prussian blue is the blue that produces the darkest greens when mixed with yellows, ochre, and permanent green.

• Combinations with sienna, reds, and umber result in very dark colors.

• Mixed with rose madder and burnt umber, Prussian blue results in black.

A

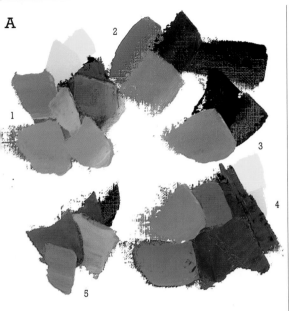

B

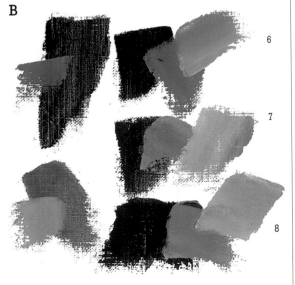

Ranges with Prussian Blue

Combining Prussian blue with another color, with or without white, and varying the proportions, produces the following ranges:

Green Range

Prussian blue mixed with yellows produces various high quality greens (1). By altering the proportions, we can obtain a range that extends from yellow-green to blue.

Blue-Green Range

This is Prussian blue with permanent green (2), and with emerald green (3); note the striking intensity of this blue-green.

These blue-greens mixed with yellows increase the range of greens to yellow-green colors (4).

The neutral range (5): Prussian blue with ochre produces greenish colors, cool if blue is predominant and warm if ochre is predominant.

Violet-Blue, Violet, and Mauve Ranges

What happens when we mix Prussian blue with red?

Look at this example with rose madder (B):

When blue is the predominant color, we get a violet-blue (6).

Violets are obtained with the appropriate proportions of Prussian blue and rose madder (7). (Remember that it is a tertiary color, so you need more rose madder than blue.)

When the mixture contains more rose madder, it acquires a mauve tendency (8).

In group B, the mixtures of violet-blues (6) are cooler. As more and more rose madder is gradually added, the tendency becomes warmer. The saturation remains the same.

MORE INFORMATION

- Prussian blue and cadmium red ranges **p. 37**
- Neutral colors **p. 47 and 49**

TITANIUM WHITE

Titanium white is opaque and very permanent. It dries more slowly than other colors.

Use of Titanium White

Titanium white is used in many color mixtures.

Whenever light tones are needed, white plays a role in the mixture. For detailed information on how to use this color correctly, see pages 56 and 57.

In these ranges graduating toward white, we can observe how the color changes from its most intense state (straight from the tube), shown in the first row, and gradually lightens.

The most intense colors have the highest degree of saturation, which is reduced by adding titanium white.

(1) Note the difference between a color in its most intense form and its least intense form. This is a tonal contrast.

(2) Note the equal intensity of two different colors. The color contrast is softened by the different tones.

(3) Note the two different colors with different degrees of intensity.

(4) Rose madder and emerald green are complementary colors. Therefore, when they are placed side by side at their maximum degree of intensity, they produce a maximum color and tonal contrast.

If we add titanium white to these mixtures, we will reduce the intensity of the colors, a fact that allows the artist to enhance the possibilities of harmonization.

Practical Applications

Any surface that can reflect light produces highlights of varying intensities. Glass, ceramics, water, and so on, even the skin of the human body (which can be shiny or matte) all reflect such highlights.

The best way to learn about this is by carrying out several comparative studies. Note what the color looks like when you squeeze it out of the tube (top row on pages 52 and 53) and compare it to the tones reproduced below. Look at the bottom row. The blended white tones are the coolest blends of all the warm colors on page 52. Compare this to the colors reproduced on page 53: The blended white tones

are the warmest blends of the cool colors on this page. Pure white is neutral and lifeless.

Returning to the subject of highlights, titanium white is the main color of any mixture. But it is not prudent to use it directly and on its own.

On pages 12 and 13 you can see how all the colors in the paintings are related, how they reflect on and off one another. Therefore, highlights are painted by toning the white with the appropriate chromatic range—that which best summarizes the influences of the surrounding colors. For example, the best way to paint a highlight on a piece of copper depends on the color of the copper and the color of the object and light that is reflected on it.

Note

Not all colors can be blended with white. Certain colors lose their identity more quickly than others.

Cadmium yellow lemon is one of the primary colors that fades.

Remember that when you add white to a color it will cool down warm colors and warm up cool ones.

MORE INFORMATION

• Light tones and pastel colors **p. 74**
• Neutral light tones and pastel colors **p. 76**

IVORY BLACK

Ivory black has a slightly warm tendency. | It is also an opaque color that is very permanent.

As you can see, white can be used to obtain a wide range of gradations.

Comparing Ivory Black with a Theoretical Black

By mixing two complementary colors in equal parts, starting out from two primary colors, you get a dark color, when toned with white, this dark color reveals that it is not really black.

Compare a "black black" with ivory black.

Should Ivory Black Be Used for Darkening Colors?

White is a color that has to be included in mixtures to obtain light colors. Black, on the other hand, does not necessarily have to be used to darken colors. The painter has the colors and the techniques to obtain an infinite number of dark tones and hues, so there is no real need to resort to black.

The deep black of ivory black produces a striking contrast when compared to the dirty black obtained by means of subtractive synthesis.

Various ways of working with dark colors

Cézanne, Young Girl Playing the Piano *(detail).*

Goya's chiaroscuros (detail).

Example of a range of blues by R. de Jesús Rodríguez (detail).

"Blacks" for Black

There are basically two types of black that can be obtained from commercially manufactured colors (A):

By combining burnt umber, emerald green, and rose madder (1), there are three possible mixtures. When you add a little white, each one of them reveals the predominance of one of the components. These "blacks," one of a rose madder tendency, another grayish, and so on, allow the painter to obtain a better harmony with the other colors of the painting.

The other mixture is made up of burnt umber, rose madder, and Prussian blue (2). With a touch of white, these blacks can take on a bluish tendency, a rose madder tendency, or a grayish tendency.

Browns and Dark Colors for "Blacks"

Why use dark colors like browns instead of black?

Because the use of such alternatives makes the contrasts less harsh than with black. Browns and dark colors can be obtained (B):

By mixing burnt umber with blue (3).

By combining burnt sienna with green (4).

Influential Blacks Enhance Gradations

All these "blacks" and browns have one thing in common: They are *influential*. The artist can obtain dark colors through a mixture that can then be adapted according to the general direction of the picture being painted. This enables the painter to produce harmonious gradations.

A

1

2

B

3

4

MORE INFORMATION

- Rose madder **p. 38**
- Burnt sienna **p. 34**
- Emerald green **p. 44**
- Prussian blue **p. 50**
- Darkening and lightening a color **p. 56**

DARKENING AND LIGHTENING A COLOR

What Is a Gradation?

A gradation is the effect achieved by gradually changing a color or tone from light to dark without any perceptible points of transition.

How can we obtain a good gradation? By paying close attention to the limits of the transitions from one color or tone to another. In a correct gradation in oils, it is essential to respect these hues. A gradation is not simply a question of adding white to lighten the color and black to darken it.

Rules for Lightening a Color

White is necessary to lighten a tone. But it must be used with the greatest of care, because not only does it lighten colors, it also grays them. Therefore, in order to lighten a color, the artist must resort to using other colors in the mixture that allow it to be illuminated and, once this has been achieved, add the minimum amount of white necessary.

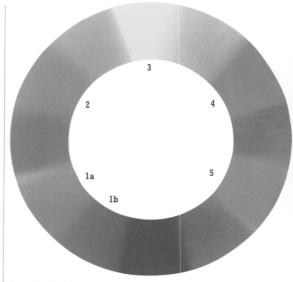

Reproduction of the colors of the light spectrum. The borders of each color band are:
(1) Blue, a. Light Blue: dark blue and blue-green.
*   b. Dark blue: light blue and violet.*
(2) Green: blue-green and yellow-green.
(3) Yellow: greenish yellow and orange-yellow.
(4) Red: dark red and orange-red.
(5) Purple: purple-red and purple-violet.
These bordering colors are shown as shades in the corresponding gradations (see examples on page 57).

Rules for Darkening a Color

Black alone conveys the complete absence of light. So, the painter requires a wide range of colors to represent the many tones that a color acquires as the light is gradually taken away from it.

A Successive Order of Tones

The simplest example of an ordered succession of tones can be demonstrated in a gradation from ivory black to titanium white.

This process is a good way of learning how to blend colors, because the same procedure is required to go from one color to another through a series of successively arranged tones. When executed correctly, the artist can express light and volume through color gradations.

In fact, any succession of perfectly arranged tones contains an infinity of colors.

Lightening and Darkening the Color of an Illuminated Object

To achieve the different degrees of illumination, we require other colors than black and white. We must use light colors to lighten and "blacks" and neutral colors to darken, especially in luminous and dim shadows that must not appear too sharp.

Yellow

10   9   8   7   6   5   4   3   2   1

The gradation from right to left:
1. White.
2. Gradually merging cadmium yellow lemon (to create a greenish hue at the border).
3. Cadmium yellow lemon is merged with cadmium yellow medium.
4. Cadmium yellow medium.
5. A little cadmium red is added to cadmium yellow medium (the darkness of the bands originates on the orange side).
6. It is darkened a little more by adding a little burnt sienna.
7. Burnt sienna.
8. The burnt sienna is darkened with rose madder.
9. The rose madder is darkened with a touch of Prussian Blue.
10. Until we reach black.

Red

7   6   5   4   3   2   1

The gradation from right to left:
1. White
2. White with a touch of cadmium red and cadmium yellow (in the part where the red turns to orange).
3. We add a little cadmium yellow with more cadmium red.
4. Cadmium red.
5. We begin adding rose madder to the cadmium red (marking the edge of the red).
6. The rose madder is darkened with Prussian blue.
7. Until we reach black.

Blue

8   7   6   5   4   3   2   1

The gradation from right to left:
1. White
2. White plus cobalt blue; the most illuminated zone is white and cobalt blue (very little) and a touch of cadmium yellow lemon at the edge of the green band).
3. Cobalt blue with very little white.
4. Cobalt blue.
5. The cobalt blue is darkened with ultramarine blue.
6. The ultramarine blue is darkened with Prussian blue.
7. Some rose madder is added to the Prussian blue (at the violet limit).
8. Until we reach black.

TRANSPARENCIES AND GLAZES

Oil is the best medium for taking advantage of glazes, layers of very transparent paint. Glazes can be applied over areas that have already been painted, whether with opaque color or impasto. The effect is very different to superimposing layers of paint. It is important to know about the transparency and opacity of oil paint if we are to use glazes effectively. You can purchase transparent, semi-opaque, and opaque colors. The application of a glaze over a dry layer of paint can be used to create interesting effects and lend luminosity to the work.

Different degrees of opacity with rose madder obtained by mixing it with white (which is very opaque). The effect of a transparent layer or glaze is evident.

Preparing a Glaze

A color prepared for application as a glaze requires plenty of medium and very little pigment. The medium is made up of equal parts of refined turpentine and linseed oil, although poppy-seed oil may be used.

We begin by preparing the medium in a palette cup and adding a little color, just enough to tint the medium while maintaining its transparent quality.

The color added to the medium can be selected from a variety of choices. The aim of the artist in adding the color is to use the glaze to alter the color over which it will be applied by making it transparent.

Theory of Color and Glazes

The painter needs to have some basic knowledge of color theory in order to know which of the already painted layers he wants to go over, and with what color glaze. Furthermore, the preceding layer must be light enough so that the glaze can be appreciated.

The color of the preceding layer is modified by means of the glaze, that is, the resulting color is the sum of the base color plus the glaze.

Important

If a glaze is applied over a freshly painted layer of color, the two will blend together, thus losing the transparent effect and dirtying the colors. Allow each layer to dry before applying a new one on top.

APPLYING A GLAZE

Glazes provide artists with another way to mix colors. Follow the procedure in example **A**: First paint a small area of orange-yellow. Then give it time to dry. Next, apply a very transparent blue glaze on top. Give it time to dry and then paint another application of the blue glaze. The greenish color obtained from a mixture of yellow and blue looks nothing like the result we have obtained with these glazes. In the area where the two glazes converge, the "green" is darker. This is the result of superimpos-

ing two layers of transparent paint.

In zone (1) of example **B**, the glaze alters all the colors that it covers, even though they are uniform and have the same color tendency.

In zone (2) we can appreciate the superimposed glaze. In the intersection, the first layer remains visible through the subsequent two glazes that were applied on top. This was carried out using ochre, emerald green, and white.

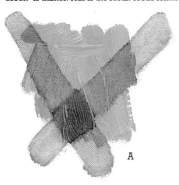

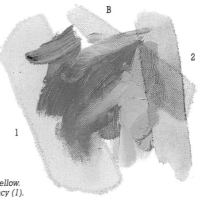

A. Two blue glazes painted over a dry layer of reddish yellow.
B. A homogenous glaze produces the same color tendency (1).
Transparencies of various superimposed colors (2).

Glaze over Textured Impasto

In addition to modifying underlying colors, glazes can also be used to highlight the relief of impasto. The plastic effects that can be achieved are truly astonishing. The artist can either play with the opacity or transparency of the first layers of color, or apply glazes of different colors over dry or wet patches.

The Drying Problem

To obtain luminous glazes, it is essential to allow each layer to dry before applying the next one. This poses a problem, however, since glazes tend to take a long time to dry. Cobalt drier is a commercial product that accelerates the drying time of oil. However, it should not be used in glazes, since it is not very transparent and would reduce significantly the amount of light given off by the glaze. Instead, try using Liquin, a product manufactured by Winsor & Newton, which is excellent for glazing and producing fine detail. If this product sits for awhile, however, it may appear discolored and won't be as free-flowing; but this should not affect its performance.

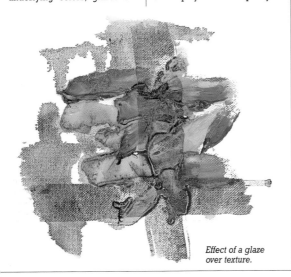

Effect of a glaze over texture.

THE FIRST APPLICATIONS

The First Dabs of Paint

The artist aims to achieve several things when he applies the first dabs of paint. It provides him with a suitable color base with which to paint fat over lean (page 15). Furthermore, the base color determines the general color scheme of the work.

If the artist works on a white canvas, the first applications are executed with a lean color so that the transparency of the paint over a white ground can help him to assess the tones of the work.

Tonal Assessment

What do we mean when we speak of tonal assessment? When we discussed the subject of gradations earlier on in this book, we spoke of the concept of a successive order of tones. Any illuminated subject acquires a

series of tonal gradations. The tonal assessment of the first applications consists of a simple sketch in oil that outlines the most essential features of the subject's tonal gradations.

Searching for the Tonal Gradation

Here are various ways of going about this task:

• The artist can gradually modify the lean color to go from the densest, darkest color to the most transparent glaze.

• The artist can apply a uniform layer of lean paint over the entire surface of the canvas. Then, using a strip cotton rag wrapped around a finger, he can "draw," thus removing the excess color in those places where there is most "light" and obtaining a sketch of the subject and its tonal gradation.

The Experienced Artist and the First Application

A preliminary application with an assessment of tones makes the painter's work that much easier. But a more experienced artist can concentrate on a freer work.

Applying a base color.

The next applications define the painting's color zones.

Tonal assessment of an apple applied with lean burnt sienna. The excess color has been removed with a strip of cotton rag.

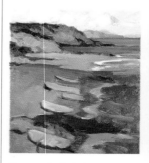

Compare the final phase of the work with the intermediate one.

Different Applications

There are several ways of applying the first colors: with different areas of color or with color washes that can be either a neutral or a specific color. A neutral application of color consists of painting one single neutral color (which may be made from a mixture of colors), and playing with various degrees of density of the color of the paint.

A cool option requires a blue color. The type of blue you would use to paint shadows will depend on the range and predominant color of the picture. It may be a violet-blue or a blue-blue (**A**). In the case of a warm tendency, the blue will have to conform to the subject's predominant color (**B**).

The artist leaves the most illuminated parts of the subject unpainted. If a cool color is required in the shadows (see page 13), the general application in a painting of a warm tendency will conform to that range in a darker tone.

These applications are neutral because they are only used to indicate the light and shadow and the general color scheme of the painting.

Specific Applications

A specific application of color, more appropriate for a large-format painting, is achieved by arranging the appropriate colors in specific areas of the canvas (**C**). These areas of color, situated within their context, allow the painter to control the outcome of the work.

Regardless of the theme, it all boils down to simplifying the areas of color, deciding which are most relevant. In this type of work, the painter concentrates on designating a color or a color mixture to each of the zones in which there is a specific or predominant color tendency.

The artist thus assesses the tones of each different color zone.

A. An initial color application in blue.

A quick sketch marking out the different zones of color.

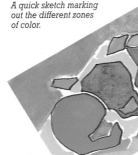

B. Here the application was effected in a warm orange tone.

C. Painting: Plein air du motard, *by M. Braunstein*

62   The First Applications
Harmonic Range of Warm Colors
Cool Colors in a Warm Range

HARMONIC RANGE OF WARM COLORS

Resolving Color Harmonies

How does the artist integrate all the color mixtures required in a painting so that they appear harmonious to the observer? This is achieved by painting a picture in a specific color range. Let's assume the general color scheme of a painting is warm. In this case, all the colors applied must tend toward this range.

In Practice

The harmonic range of warm colors comprises all the color mixtures of warm colors, with or without white, including the earth colors. A picture painted with a harmonic range of warm colors acquires a general reddish tendency.

The predominance of warm colors does not necessarily exclude the use of cool colors (present in mixtures for violets and yellow-greens). Cool color mixtures are necessary for painting shadows, or for toning certain

mixtures that are too pure.

Cooler mixtures do not reduce the general warm tendency of the whole; indeed, they enhance the painting and can be used to create contrasts.

In order to obtain harmonious colors within the same range, the artist need only add small quantities of the other colors to the general color, or the predominant color.

Nonetheless, even a perfect color harmony can become monotonous. Therefore, many painters include dramatic contrasts in order to highlight the predominant color range.

Warm Colors with a Predominant Color

This involves painting with a palette containing a harmonic range of warm colors and mixtures that all tend toward a predominant color. For instance, if the predominant color is orange, the artist has to ensure that all the color mixtures he uses in his work tend toward this color.

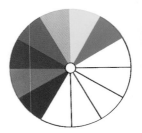

Theoretical diagram
This diagram shows how warm colors are basically made up of purple, magenta, dark red, red, orange, yellow, and light green.

How to Adjust the Color Mixtures in a Warm Palette

Let's examine the colors obtained by mixing warm colors together (yellows, reds, and earth colors), with or without white. In each of the swatches of colors we can see the colors used to obtain them and their mixtures:

• The combination of cadmium yellow lemon and cadmium yellow medium with white, and a brushstroke of cadmium red, more orange in tone. This stroke illustrates how the yellows can be "warmed" by adding a little red. In a warm range, cadmium yellow medium is useful because it can be used to quickly obtain an orange tonality (1).

• These are mixtures of yellow with red and white (2). The hues they can take on are shown in 3 and 4.

• Mixtures of reds with cadmium yellow lemon and white (3).

• Mixtures of reds with cadmium yellow medium and white (4).

Note how the mixtures in 3 are cooler than those of 4, due to the quality of each yellow. Likewise, it is important to know which red is more suitable in a mixture.

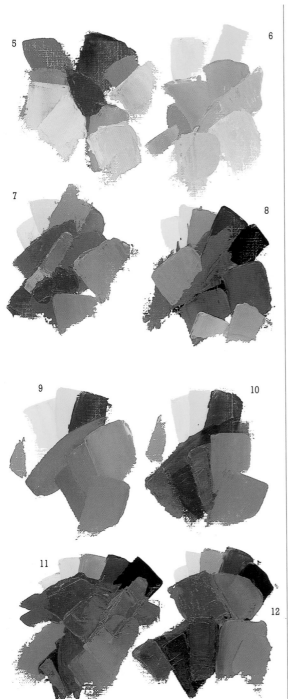

• Mixtures with reds: cadmium red and rose madder with white. Starting with intense reds, note how as you add white the color lightens and at the same time "cools." By adding very little yellow, in addition to the white, we can maintain the harmony (5).

• Yellow mixtures containing ochre and white (6) produce the same effect as in the examples in (8): They lack the warmth seen in the other examples.

• These are mixtures of yellows, ochres, and reds with white (7). In fact, they are the result of adding red to the mixtures of 6. They clearly produce a warmer harmony.

• From a combination of yellows with earth colors, sienna, and umber, plus white, we obtain a duller group for a warm palette (8).

The following mixtures show how it is possible to use earth colors in a way that, when combined with other colors, we can obtain dark colors that are intensely warm. In this case, a touch of red is always required.

• Mixtures of yellows, ochre, sienna, and cadmium red, plus white (9). These are darker and duller mixtures than in 3 and 4, but are warm.

• Mixtures of yellows, sienna, and rose madder with white. The result is several dark mixtures that convey a real sensation of warmth (10).

• Starting with cadmium red and mixing it with yellow and earth colors, with or without white, we can obtain a group of frankly harmonious and warm colors (11).

• Starting out with rose madder and mixing it with yellow and earth colors, we obtain several ranges of tones that are different than those in 11, but that are equally pleasant to look at (12).

MORE INFORMATION

• Harmonic range of cool colors **p. 64**

COOL COLORS IN A WARM RANGE

Cool Colors and a Warm Palette

Theoretically, yellow-green and violet are present in the range of warm colors.

In practice, in order to obtain these colors, we must include cool colors in our palette, in such situations as when a green has to be a warm yellow-green, or the violets require a warm tendency. The artist must choose, therefore, the right colors to successfully obtain this effect. The mixtures demonstrated on these pages must be harmonized with the warm range.

Before studying the mixtures between warm and cool colors required to paint shadows, enhance tones, or create a contrast in a warm palette, let's first examine how different problems are solved according to general rules.

Different Solutions

In the painting by Cassat, the tiny strokes of color in the child's neckerchief do not break with the warm harmony of the painting. The cool colors have been used to tone warm colors. In the still life work, the bold outlines, which contrast with complementary colors and the concentrated nucleus of greens, create a truly coloristic result.

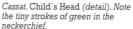

Cassat. Child's Head *(detail). Note the tiny strokes of green in the neckerchief.*

Esther Olivé de Puig. Cool colors used to create contrast in a predominantly warm painting (fragment).

A

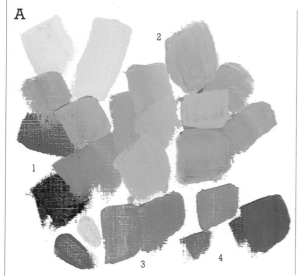

A. Mixtures of yellows with greens and white

With cadmium yellow lemon and greens, we obtain yellow-greens of a cool tendency (1).

Cadmium yellow medium and greens produce yellow-greens (2) that are warmer than those in group 1.

Note how the greens behave with ochre: The yellow-greens are now golden and warm (3).

A touch of red or rose madder added to any yellow-green is enough to warm it. Thus we obtain earth colors that can be used to tone shadows (4).

Bearing in mind that red and green are complementary colors, they must be mixed in unequal proportions.

Compare **A** with **B**.

B

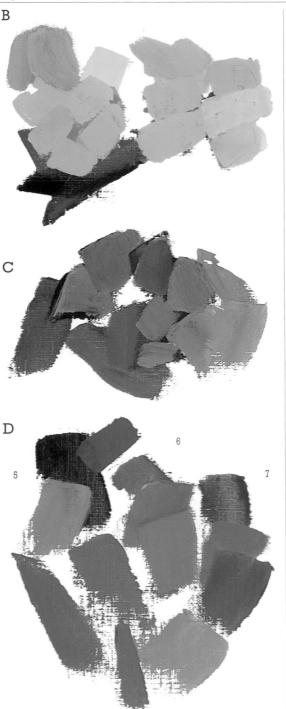

B. Mixtures between blues and cadmium yellow medium with white

To obtain yellow-greens, we require abundant yellow and very little blue. The tiny quantities of blue must be added to the main color, which in this case is warm.

It is worth remembering that mixtures with cobalt blue are warmer. Just as in **A** (p. 64), we can warm the color a little more by adding a little red.

MORE INFORMATION

- Ranges with permanent green **p. 43**
- Ranges with emerald green **p. 45**

C

C. For violets and purples

By blending together reds and blues with white, we obtain mixtures of a warm tendency, the best examples being violet colors of a reddish or rose madder tendency. These colors are mainly used to paint or tone shadows.

Conclusion

Given that small quantities of cool colors are used in the mixtures in **A**, **B**, and **C**, we can conclude that to obtain the right cool color mixtures for use with warm colors, we have to add tiny amounts of blue or green to the main color.

D

5

6

7

D. Ranges of purple and violet

Using a commercially manufactured violet on the palette is very handy for enhancing the range of violets and purples.

Violet can be appreciated in two tones by mixing it with white, and as it gradually warms, reds and white are added little by little to the mixtures (5).

With cadmium red (6).

With rose madder (7).

66 Cool Colors in a Warm Range
Harmonic Range of Cool Colors
Warm Colors in a Cool Range

HARMONIC RANGE OF COOL COLORS

Harmonic Range of Cool Colors

The colors that are used in a painting conform to a specific range that makes it aesthetically pleasing to the observer. In this case, we are going to examine the predominant use of cool colors to paint a picture.

Theoretical Diagram

This diagram shows the harmonic range of cool colors comprising light green, green, dark green, cyan blue, ultramarine blue, intense blue, and violet.

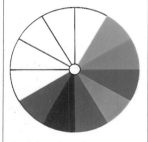

A color wheel showing the range of cool colors.

Warm Colors in Cool Paintings

Warm colors can be used in many ways with cool colors. Here the warm colors produce a sharp contrast with the cool range of blues. Esther Olivé de Puig

The presence of warm colors in this predominantly cool range allows the inclusion of subtle shadows without harsh contrasts. Josep Sala.

The Cool Range of Colors in Practice

In practice, this range includes all the mixtures between cool colors with or without white. The general tendency of all these mixtures is cool, that is, they are bluish in tone.

Red can also be included in the cool range of colors. However, it must be added in a harmonious way with or without white. Given that the main color is cool, tiny amounts of red are enough to obtain suitable mixtures for the range. It is important, however, not to forget the problems of mixing complementary colors together.

These "warmed" cool mixtures allow the artist to add contrasts to the general color tendency in order to enhance the work.

Warm colors can be included in a painting of a cool tendency in a variety of ways.

Cool Colors

We can mix cool colors together with or without white. In each group, **A**, **B**, and **C**, we can see the main colors and their mixtures.

Combining permanent green with emerald green plus white (**A**). Emerald green can be used to obtain a much cooler range with white. These bluish greens harmonize with the mixtures of **B**.

A combination of greens and blues, with white (B). Among the blues used are cobalt blue, ultramarine blue, and Prussian blue; the greens include emerald green and a permanent green.

A

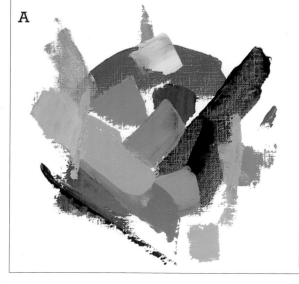

Cool Colors in a Warm Range
Harmonic Range of Cool Colors
Warm Colors in a Cool Range

67

B

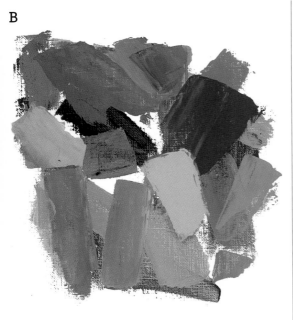

C

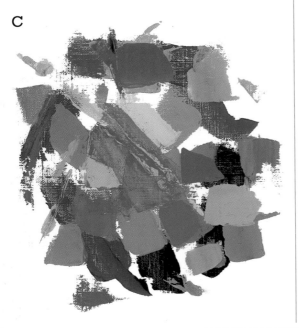

Pause for a moment to consider the delicate harmony of this group of mixtures.

If we produce mixtures of greens and blues with a decidedly blue tendency, we get several magnificent, intense blue-greens. We would, therefore, obtain more swatches with contrast than in **C**.

We can also consider creating mixtures of greens and blues of a predominantly green tendency. In this case we can increase the range of examples in **A**.

By combining blues together with white, we obtain a wide range of blues (**C**). Note the interplay of textures and transparencies.

Having examined the three color groups **A**, **B**, and **C**, we can see the harmony of the whole.

Comment

The picture of the boats on page 66 was executed quickly, in two phases.

The first phase involved situating the main zones of color, the boats, the lines of the composition, the water, the horizon line, and sky. All of this was painted in an exquisite cool blue range, in which we can easily make out the color mixtures in groups **A**, **B**, and **C**.

Note, in addition, the minimum touches of warm color included in the work.

The second phase of this work entailed painting in the reflections.

MORE INFORMATION

· Warm colors in a cool range **p. 68**

WARM COLORS IN A COOL RANGE

Warm Colors in a Cool Palette?

How can we use warm colors in a cool palette? It is a question of mixing them with the right colors and in the correct proportions in order to obtain mixtures that are harmonious with the cool range.

First we paint the cool base color and then blend the most suitable warm colors with it. In theory, we require yellow-greens and violets that, when applied correctly, can be harmonized with a cool range of colors.

In Practice

All mixtures must conform to the predominant color of the painting. One simple way of ensuring this is to add tiny quantities of the chosen colors to the predominant color.

Examples

The artists who painted these two pictures avoided harsh contrasts by creating subtle harmonies of cool colors.

Thanks to the extensive central light zone, the figure stands out from the background in a subtle and harmonious manner. Badía Camps.

The brushwork of warm colors applied over a blue background creates a nebulous middle ground, a characteristic impressionist technique, without sharp contrasts. Miquel Ferrón.

A

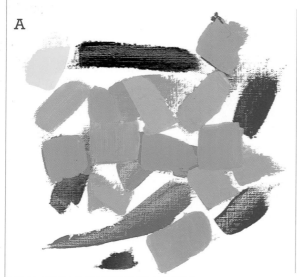

Mixing Cool and Warm Colors

Let's examine some mixtures. **A** and **B** are typical mixtures, while the mixtures in **C** have been obtained for a specific purpose.

Yellow-greens (A). Combining yellow with either green or blue lends the mixtures a cooler quality. Cadmium yellow lemon with emerald green produces yellow-greens that are perfect for use in a cool palette.

Compare these results with the yellow-green examples for a warm palette (see p. 64).

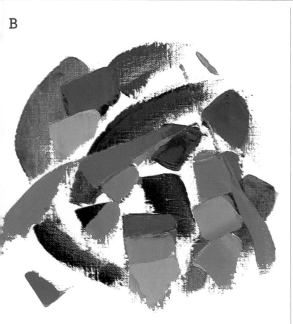

B

How to use the violet range in a cool palette. This is done by mixing rose madder with blues and white. It is essential to add just the right amount of blue to ensure that the mixture attains a cool tendency (**B**).

Violet-Greens

It is easy to create a violet-blue, but how do we go about obtaining the violet-greens so common in landscapes of a bluish tendency?

We turn our attention to mixture **C**. Green is obtained by mixing yellow and blue together; the only way to create the violet hue is by adding rose madder, and that means combining complementary colors.

So, the violet-greens that exist in nature must be obtained with unequal proportions of either color. The results are exquisite hues.

Compare the result of the mixtures of **C** with those of **B**. The subtle change of hue in **C** indicates that a tiny quantity of the complementary color has been added.

The Aim of Color Mixtures

The aim of these color mixtures—**A**, **B**, and **C**—has been to create a harmony, obtaining colors without harsh contrasts that can be used to paint a picture in the range of cool colors.

Whether the artist wants to create a subtle harmony without sharp contrasts or, on the other hand, to obtain a subjective balance of chromatic contrasts depends on her sensitivity and vision of the theme. The artist's aim will determine the type of mixtures she requires.

C

MORE INFORMATION

· Yellow-greens **p. 64**
· Purple and violets **p. 65**
· Possible subjects **p. 84**

HARMONIC RANGE OF NEUTRAL COLORS 1

Neutral Color

A neutral color is obtained by mixing two complementary colors in unequal proportions, with or without white.

Harmonic Range of Neutral Colors

The harmonic range of neutral colors is composed of mixtures obtained from pairs of complementary colors. The choice of complementary colors depends on the subject you want to paint.

The Color of a Picture Painted with Neutral Colors

A neutral color—a mixture of complementary colors—contains something of the three primary colors. Due to the effect of subtractive synthesis, if we mix any two complementary colors together in equal parts we get a dark blackish color. When the proportions of the colors are blended in unequal parts, they become a gray version of the predominant color in the mixture.

Therefore, a picture painted exclusively with neutral colors acquires a grayish appearance. The colors appear dirty, especially when compared with pure cool or warm colors.

How to Choose Pairs of Complementary Colors

Each composition requires its own specific range of colors. Let's examine some possible options:

1. The color wheel shows us the complementary colors, which are diametrically opposed to one another. So, the complementary colors run thus: rose madder and green, cyan blue and red, yellow and dark blue, yellow-green and violet, orange and violet-blue, blue-green and carmine red.

2. In practice, the examples of mixtures we have been studying indicate the degree of complementariness of the standard colors with one another.

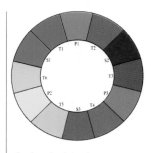

A color wheel showing complementary colors diametrically opposed to one another. Primary colors (P), secondary colors (S), and tertiary colors (T).

3. Standard colors can be used to obtain complementary colors; then by mixing them in unequal proportions and adding white, neutral colors are created. The diagram included in this section will come in very handy for this purpose: for instance, by combining yellow and red together we obtain orange, the complementary color of ultramarine blue.

4. Any standard neutral color mixed with another produces neutral colors. All earth colors are neutral (see page 26). Mixing an earth color with another standard color produces another neutral color, which itself is a mixture of complementary colors, although in different proportions.

Note: This graphic reproduction allows us to see the types of colors we are dealing with.

Two Tendencies

Each pair of complementary colors we choose produces colors that can be grouped into two tendencies, depending on which color is the predominant color of the mixture.

For example, we first choose two complementary colors, rose madder and emerald green. Then we mix them together in unequal parts. Now let's see what else we can do with them (see p. 71).

In **A** the predominant color of this neutral mixture is rose madder.

In **B** the predominant color is emerald green.

Now we will produce mixtures between primary colors that can be used to create neutral colors. See what combinations can be created by mixing rose madder, cadmium yellow lemon, and Prussian blue:

C is a blue range with a predominant blue.

D is a rose madder range with a predominant rose madder.

Working with Neutral Colors

It is essential for the artist to become familiar with complementary colors and the colors that can be used to create complementary colors.

One way of learning is to imagine a color reduced to its theoretical composition of primary colors. For instance, ochre has a decidedly yellow tendency. This is useful to bear in mind for all mixtures containing ochre.

Practical palette work allows the painter to gain more in-depth knowledge of the subtleties of the neutral range of colors.

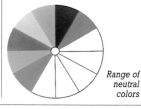

Range of neutral colors

Neutral Colors with Earth Colors

When we mix an earth color with another standard color, the result is yet another neutral color, as we can see in the mixtures with ochre and sienna (**E** and **F**).

If we now combine yellow ochre and ultramarine blue with white, we obtain neutral colors of either a bluish or an ochre tendency (**E**).

A neutral color with a predominant blue tendency (**1**).

Color (**1**) with white added to it (**2**).

The neutral color has an ochre tendency (**3**).

Color (**3**) in which ochre predominates over blue, mixed with white (**4**).

These colors were created using burnt sienna and emerald green with a few touches of white in the lightest parts (**F**).

Here we can observe:

A neutral color with a predominant sienna tendency (**5**).

Color (**5**) with white added to it (**6**).

The color with an emerald green tendency (**7**).

Color (**7**) with white added to it (**8**).

The range that can be developed from **E** and **F**, when mixed correctly, can produce colors of exceptional beauty and exceptional harmony.

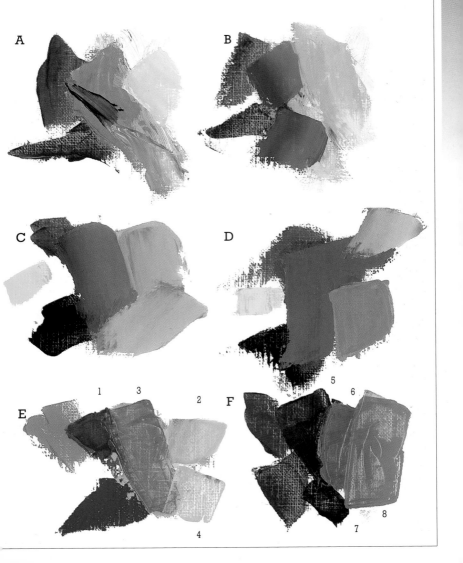

HARMONIC RANGE OF NEUTRAL COLORS 2

Grays

It requires plenty of practice to be able to mix complementary colors and keep the degree of grayness under control.

Pause for a moment and study the wealth of hues that the artist has created with gray and blue neutral colors in this painting.

The tiny hints of red and white provide a touch of interesting variety to the theme.

This work by Marta Durán, painted with several layers of paint and thick impasto, clearly demonstrates how an artist can master the "art" of grays.

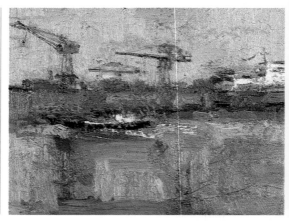

More Neutral Color Applications

Here are mixtures obtained using the color wheel.

By combining red and yellow, you obtain an orange color (**A**), which is the complementary color of ultramarine blue (or violet-blue). Observe:

In the neutral color in which orange predominates, the tendency is greenish ochre (**1**).

In the neutral color in which blue is predominant, the tendency is toward a dark green (**2**).

It is interesting to compare these examples to those of group **E** on page 71. They are similar. There is abundant yellow in the ochre, a little red, and just a dash of blue. If blue is added to the ochre, we obtain the same mix as in (**1**).

Yellow-green, whether standard or a mixture (the result of a combination of green and yellow), is the complementary color of standard violet or a mixture of rose madder and Prussian blue (**B**). With this pair of complementary colors we discover that:

The neutral color can either be predominantly green (**3**) or predominantly violet (**4**).

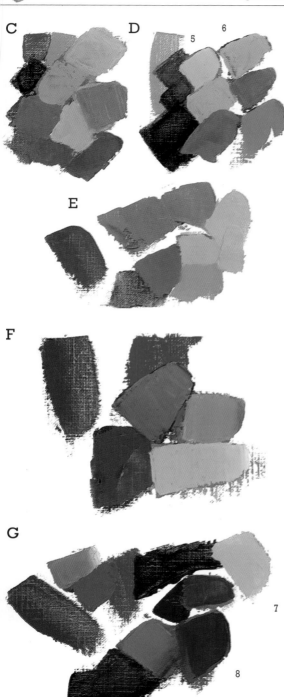

In-depth Information on the Subject

Neutral colors mixed with other colors provide an unlimited range of neutral hues.

To illustrate this point, let's examine several examples of neutral colors mixed with blues, and also with greens.

We create our neutral colors with rose madder and ochre (for a dirty red), with blues (cobalt, ultramarine, and Prussian) and white (**C**): By including all the differences of each blue, we obtain an interesting and wide range.

Now we mix ochre with blues and white (**D**):

It is the ochre that predominates in this color (**5**).

Now the blue predominates (**6**).

Moving on to burnt sienna, we can see the differences in hue between the neutral colors of one or another green tendency, and between those of a predominant sienna tendency. The mixtures together (**E**) are truly harmonic.

The next test involves studying the ranges that can be produced with burnt sienna and blues (**F** and **G**):

Sienna and cobalt blue (**F**).

Sienna and ultramarine blue (**7**).

Sienna and Prussian blue (**8**).

Mixtures with a blue or even a sienna predominance convey the impression of a highly complete harmony.

Proportion of Mixtures of Complementary Colors

We recommend mixing complementary colors in unequal parts in order to obtain cleaner and less gray neutral colors. But when painting requires very dark colors, the difference between the proportion of one color and its complementary color is reduced.

MORE INFORMATION

- Harmonic range of neutral colors 1 **p. 70**
- Neutral light tones and pastel colors **p. 76**

LIGHT TONES AND PASTEL COLORS

Light Tones and Warm Pastel Colors

White is used in a mixture whenever it is necessary to obtain a very light or pale tone. Reproduced on this page is a wide variety of examples of soft, subdued light tones of a warm tendency.

The artist can create a pastel tone from any warm color mixture. Simply by mixing abundant white with a small amount of a warm color will do the job. When the standard warm colors we are using in this book (cadmium yellow lemon, cadmium yellow medium, cadmium red, rose madder, and earth colors) are mixed with one another, and abundant white is then added, we can obtain these warm pastel colors.

Increasing the Palette

By adding more standard warm colors to the palette, we increase the possibilities for mixtures with different tones and hues. *(For example, Naples yellow, terra rosa transparent, carmine lake, permanent pink, and so on.)*

Light Tones and Cool Pastel Colors

The examples reproduced on this page are pastel tones of a cool tendency.

Regardless of its makeup, a cool pastel tone can be obtained by adding plenty of white. Cool colors contain greens and blues.

These mixtures contain two greens: permanent green and emerald green, and three blues: cobalt blue, ultramarine blue, and Prussian blue, all of which have had lots of white added to them in order to produce pale cool tones.

Toned Down Contrast

It is evident that the contrasts and harshness of light tones are reduced to such an extent that, although they are different ranges, these color mixtures still appear highly harmonious even when they are placed next to each other.

Expressiveness of Pastel Tones

As indicated on page 10, light colors and pastel tones are used to convey such a delicate and soft harmony that a picture composed entirely of pastel tones has a congenial and delicate atmosphere. The next chapter examines how it is possible to obtain a similar effect using neutral colors.

NEUTRAL LIGHT TONES AND PASTEL COLORS

Neutral Colors and Colors of a Warm Tendency

White, in large quantities, is the color used to obtain each one of the examples reproduced below. For each color to be considered neutral, a pair of complementary colors must be included in unequal parts. The predominant color of each mixture is white, but the warm tendency the color gives off corresponds to the complementary color that dominates the mixture.

The examples on this page are neutral colors of a warm tendency. Some were created with standard neutral colors, others through mixtures of complementary colors, with a predominant warm color, having added plenty of white to them all.

It is interesting to compare these examples with the ones on page 74. Close observation reveals that these mixtures of neutral tones appear "dirty," and have less vitality. This is due to the presence of the respective complementary color. Though included in only a small proportion, it still manages to "muddy" the result.

Neutral Tones and Colors of a Cool Tendency

The colors on this page are examples of light neutral tones of a cool tendency.

Regardless of the pair of complementary colors used in a mixture, the cooler color always predominates.

The largest proportion of color used is white. The combinations of complementary colors are added in tiny amounts.

The tendency of these colors is bluish, greenish, or gray, depending on the predominant tone.

If we compare the two groups of neutral colors on this page and the previous page, we can immediately recognize each tone's tendency.

Since they are neutral, the mixture of complementary colors in unequal parts reduces the contrasts significantly. Furthermore, the large amount of white used in each mixture, which cools the warm colors and warms the cool ones, reduces the contrast even further.

Note the extreme delicacy of the colors on these two pages.

Using light tones and pastel colors of a neutral tendency allows the painter to create exquisite color harmony.

White "Grays"

White tends to gray when added to color. The painter normally has a large tube of white, because greater quantities are required of it than of any other color of the palette.

White must always be used with great care in mixtures because it not only lightens them, but also, in most cases, grays them.

FLESH COLORS

The Range of Flesh Colors Depends on the Chosen Palette

Before artists embark on a painting of the human figure, they should choose the most suitable flesh tones within the color range they have selected.

There Is No Single Flesh Color

The term "flesh color" refers to the way we represent the human skin in a painting. There is no single flesh color. The color of a person's skin depends on various characteristics, such as whether it is white or black, pale or rosy, wrinkled or smooth, shiny, and so on. The color of human flesh also depends to a great extent on the lighting, for example, whether we see the person in daylight, by electric light, and so forth.

Gauguin, Two Tahitian Women *(detail).*

Flesh Color Theory

We should see flesh color as a gradation—in other words, look at the brightest points of the skin as they gradually decrease in light, until they are in shadow.

Observation

Dark or brown skin, even when well illuminated, requires the inclusion of a greater number of mixtures of rose madder and blue than white skin in the same lighting conditions. The typical color of dark skin always contains some blue.

Avoiding Sharp Contrasts

When painting a human figure it is essential to know how to avoid creating contrasts that are too sharp; the artist must ensure that the mixtures applied next to one another, blended or not, comply with a coherent tonal gradation, because abrupt tonal changes in human skin are psychologically more unacceptable than those of an object.

Which Color?

Remember that we can obtain any color by mixing yellow, red, and blue and adding white. Therefore, we must define the flesh color of our subject by adapting it to the particular lighting conditions. In practice, it all boils down to choosing the right yellow, red, and blue and blending them in correct proportions.

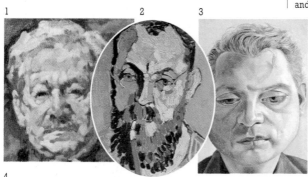

Composition. There is no single flesh color.

1. Franz Rederer, Herbert Louis Samuel *(detail).*

2. André Derain, Portrait of Henri Matisse *(detail).*

3. Lucian Freud, Francis Bacon *(detail).*

4. Sir Stanley Spencer, Self-Portrait *(detail).*

5. Walter Sickert, William Maxwell Aitken *(detail).*

6. Picasso, Life *(detail).*

Certain Predominant Colors Used for Painting Flesh

Let's examine some paintings by well-known artists:

1. Frank Benson, Portrait of My Daughters (detail). This is a warm scene; all the colors used are warm: the backlit areas tend toward yellow, and the areas lit by full sunlight tend toward very light pink.

2. Mary Cassat, Mother and Boy. Another warm painting, this time an interior, which gives off a golden and pinkish, less luminous color.

3. Cézanne, The Card Players. The faces of the players have a markedly warm tendency.

4. Robert Reid, Fleur-de-Lys. The predominant tendency is blue and violet-blue. Pay close attention to how the flesh has been painted with cool colors.

5. Frank Benson, Sunlight. There are many aspects of this magnificent work to comment on, but we will concentrate on its range of flesh colors. The artist has achieved a contrast between its zones of illuminated warm colors and the cool and luminous shadows with utmost dexterity.

6. Frederick Frieseke, The Bird Cage. This painting's range of colors produces an extraordinary backlit effect.

7. Frederick Frieseke, Summer. A splendid use of colors to obtain shadow.

All Colors Can Be Used as Flesh Colors

Flesh colors can be represented with almost any color. A good example of this can be found in this work by Boccioni, in which the model's skin color is painted with an infinity of colors.

His study of light, which integrates the figure into the surroundings, is achieved by means of extraordinary backlighting.

Boccioni, Bust of His Mother.

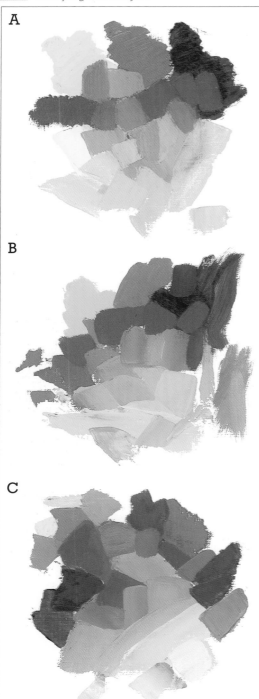

A

B

C

Warm Ranges of Flesh Colors

Let's look at three groups of warm colors. An overall study of these examples will allow us to establish some very useful guidelines.

The first point to remember is that all of these mixtures require plenty of white.

We will begin with mixtures of cadmium yellow lemon with reds and white, which we will gradually darken by adding a little ochre (**A**).

We can obtain more pinkish mixtures, some of a carmine tendency, and other luminous tones of cooler tendency, due to the characteristic lemon tendency of the yellow used.

Now we add cadmium yellow medium with reds and white, and gradually include a little ochre to darken the mixture and create duller tones. The general tendency of these examples is toward orange, even rosy pink in the light tones (**B**).

If we combine a range of ochres (ochre with yellows) with reds and white, we begin to see a touch of blue in the mixture. This is because ochre is obtained with abundant yellow, a touch of rose madder, and a hint of blue. The flesh color now begins to darken (**C**).

Summary

Cadmium yellow lemon produces a luminous cool tendency; cadmium yellow medium produces a reddish-yellow tendency; ochre produces a duller but golden tendency; cadmium red produces a reddish tendency; and rose madder a carmine tendency.

It is essential to bear in mind the characteristics of each standard yellow and red when painting a figure with a range of warm colors, and to plan the mixtures accordingly.

Earth colors such as ochre and sienna, used sensibly (that is, in very tiny amounts), allow the artist to tone down flesh colors that appear too pure. Their presence in the mixture lends the flesh color its vital touch of credibility. Of course, they are also used to create tonal changes. In order to obtain darker tones, we must gradually add darker earth colors.

Cool Flesh Colors

If we were working with a cool range of colors, we would have to paint the flesh with colors that harmonized with the general cool color scheme of the picture. In the painting *Fleur-de-Lys*, the flesh colors were obtained using white, blue, and rose madder (see page 79). Another fine example of cool flesh colors can be seen in this work by Picasso.

The Color of Flesh in Shadow

In order to paint a shadow you can add blue—which is present in all shadows—or darken the same color, or you can even mix it with its complementary color. Depending on the range chosen and the wish to dramatize or contrast light and shadow, the painter will increase the effect of shadows, thus minimizing the colors and using just one of the techniques described in order to enhance them.

Page 80 provides a graphic example of how to darken warm flesh colors using sienna and ochre.

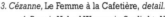

1. Picasso, Life.

2. Gauguin, Two Tahitian Women on the Beach, detail of the face.

3. Cézanne, Le Femme à la Cafetière, detail.

4. Renoir, Naked Woman in Sunlight. Note the greenish patches on the woman's body.

5. Degas, Head of a Young Woman, detail. The greenish hues of the flesh color are also used to paint the shadows, establishing an optimum relationship between background and figure.

D

E

Let's study an example of a warm flesh color in a cool shadow with a greenish tendency (**D** and **E**).

Ochre and cadmium yellow medium are mixed with permanent green and white (1).

The same mixture is carried out, but cadmium yellow medium is used instead of cadmium yellow lemon (2). We darken the mixtures with burnt sienna (3).

Here ochre is mixed with cadmium yellow medium and emerald green plus white (4).

The same colors are used again, except that the yellow is now cadmium yellow lemon (5). If in 3 the aim is to darken the mixtures with sienna, in 6 the sienna is darkened by adding a little blue, until we obtain umber. These are colors that allow us to darken combinations gradually.

STUDYING THE SUBJECT

Simplifying and Arranging

It all boils down to simplifying and organizing the most essential aspects of the theme. Once you have decided on the structure and composition, you should study the whole and find the best way to develop it. A study of a subject always begins with its most significant masses of color.

Squinting Your Eyes to Search for the Most Significant Masses of Color

By observing something through squinted eyes, we can make out its most obvious parts. We won't see anything in detail, but we can reduce the theme to its essential features. Even though the artist cannot make out the details (houses, figures, trees, and so on), he can perceive the intensities of light, the basic tones, and the most important color masses.

Confronted with a white canvas, the painter must fill the space with color. By squinting his eyes, he can identify the most significant color zones, and simplify the forms that occupy the space.

The Seine and Notre Dame

The subject, a well-focused photograph revealing all the details and light and shadows.

The same subject, this time seen through squinted eyes. (It is the same scene, but out of focus.)

Procedure

Simplifying essential aspects of a theme allows the painter to establish zones of color and tone. It permits him to determine the optimum relationship between colors and the best way to harmonize them, all of which lends the painting coherence. All the color mixtures a painter uses must conform to the color ranges he has selected to paint the work in, as well as to the type of atmosphere he wishes to create.

Synthesizing and Detailing

The artist always paints in two ways. She reduces the subject to its most essential forms or features and then adds details, continuously alternating between the two. With a few brushstrokes, the painter roughs out basic forms. Then she adds a few details to make the form clearer. The way in which the artist chooses to balance these two tasks is a purely personal matter.

Reducing the Subject to Its Most Basic Features

On the one hand, we must distribute the basic and most important lines of the theme on the canvas. This calls for determining the right structure and studying its composition.

It is the structure that defines the limits of each color mass. Then, it is a matter of finding a way to relate the different color zones to obtain a coherent whole.

AN EXAMPLE OF SYNTHESIS

Sketch: the main lines that define the space, assigning one zone to each element.

The previous sketch with the zones numbered.

Observations

The Sky

The best way to paint the sky is with a gradation of gray tones, starting at the top with the darkest one and gradually lightening toward the horizon, behind the buildings (1).

In this case, the most intense light is an orange tone located around the trees on the right (2).

The River

There are six major tones that can easily be made out. They are numbered from the most luminous to the most dark (3), (4), (5), (6), (7), (8), (9).

The Buildings

The bridge and riverbanks are the structures that contain the most significant contrasts of light and shadow. The darkest elements are the edges between the embankment and the water, the steps, and the area below the bridge: (10), (11), (12), (13), (14), (15). See the shaded sketch below.

The building on the left (16) is the pinkest of all.

For this type of subject, it is important to bear in mind the question of perspective. It is essential that the lines that convey the structure of the buildings, bridge, and riverbanks conform to a coherent perspective.

The sensation of depth is vital for correctly representing a three-dimensional subject on canvas.

In this example of a Parisian landscape, the maximum sensation of depth can only be achieved with a correct representation of the sky, together with accurate vanishing lines and good color harmony. The best way to capture this is through a colored drawing.

This method allows the artist to choose the harmonic range that will predominate in the work. A neutral palette appears to be most suitable for this subject. See pages 70 to 73.

Partial sketch: the most significant dark zones of the bridge and the riverbank.

POSSIBLE SUBJECTS

The Inspired Artist

What makes an artist want to paint a specific subject? Sometimes it is because the subject has an attractive setting. On other occasions, it may be the placement of the objects in the composition that attracts the artist. More often than not, it is the infinite chromatic possibilities that inspire the artist to paint.

When the Subject Suggests Itself

A study of a potential subject allows us to see if there is a coherent color relationship between its basic elements. Some subjects "suggest themselves" to the artist, due to their attractive colors, others by meeting the artist's personal criteria. The choice of color range will guide the artist in all the mixtures he produces to paint his work.

The Choice of a Subject

Here are a few examples of subjects with a specific range of colors.

Photographs of subjects for painting with warm colors.

Bouquet of flowers of a warm chromatic range.

The red city.

Photographs of subjects for painting with cool colors.

Landscape with river.

Green and blue-green landscape.

Blue landscape.

Photographs of subjects for painting with neutral colors.

A beach.

A landscape on a misty day.

THE ARTIST CHOOSES

If you brought a group of artists together and asked them all to paint the same subject, each painting would be different.

When an artist decides to paint the subject as it appears in nature, she uses the appropriate palette, the one that best represents the predominant color of the theme. But if the painter decides to make it appear more dramatic, for instance, the color scheme she uses to establish her own particular vision of the theme is in her head. The painter's aim in this case is to make the subject appear as she wants it to be seen.

Compare the photographs of the subjects and the pictures painted.

Photographs of subjects painted by Esther Olivé de Puig.

Compare the difference between Puig's painting and the original.

Personal Interpretation

Depending on the subject and the type of expressiveness the artist wishes to impose on it, she can choose the most harmonic method or one providing greater contrast.

A Personal Creation

We know that to harmonize is to establish a good relationship between the colors of a painting, with the aim of making the whole appear pleasing to the eye. According to this definition, any harmonized work is a personal creation.

Among the swatches of colors, a contrast by tone or color can be created whose maximum contrast is produced between intense complementary colors. In order to exploit contrast, it is essential to understand and know how to get the most out of complementary colors.

Two adjacent colors that are opposite on the color wheel complement one another in a way that produces a form of contrast in the painting. When executed in a way convenient to the general structure of the painting, contrasts produce a balanced effect.

Conclusion

In a subjective way, each artist develops a balance between harmonization and contrast according to what he wants to express.

EXPRESSION AND CONTRAST

Expressive Aspect

The symbolism and psychology of color is concentrated in the areas of harmonization and contrast:

(a) If we want to create a delicate, passive, and subdued atmosphere, the picture must be painted with pastel colors, which have neither contrasts nor intensity.

(b) A lively, dynamic atmosphere, on the other hand, requires contrasted colors of intense tones.

But, (a) and (b) are not the only options. We can establish an infinite number of chromatic balances.

Expressing Contrasts

There are natural contrasts, such as that between this brightly colored macaw and the green vegetation of the background. But the artist is free to create contrasts. That is exactly what the Postimpressionist and the Fauvist movements did: heighten contrasts between complementary colors to the maximum.

Note that maximum contrasts can be obtained by juxtaposing complementary colors. This subject was painted solely through contrast. The result of this technique is astonishing. Though we accept this form of artistic expression nowadays, in its own day many artists staunchly criticized this style. They would ask—understandably—how it was possible for a person to be painted with

Use of complementary color. André Derain. Portrait of Henri Matisse.

green skin. Today, we accept the possibility of exalting, dramatizing, and exaggerating with color. Let's examine some colorist works by M. Braunstein.

The Power of Color

The Little Red Bicycle. This painting was inspired by a child's bicycle standing in the undergrowth in a park. The color scheme may appear aggressive because so many pure and complementary colors are included, but the idea was to convey an energy, vitality, and force that moved the painter. Regardless of motive, that was what the painter wanted to transmit.

The dramatization of shadows. Anyone with normal sight sees things in more or less the same way. But what we see means different things to different people. Shadows may appear magical to some, a fact that gives rise to countless possibilities. We can, for instance, include contrasting colors in the color of a shadow (see page 13).

An autumn landscape. The trees look genuinely radiant. This typically colorist approach is daring, although the result is

undeniably attractive. This is an energetic, even aggressive work.

The exaltation of reflections. The reflections and highlights on any surface can be exaggerated. The chromatic possibilities in this field allow the artist to achieve a

Macaw

sensation of depth and volume. The first example is with ceramic. The second is with varnished wood and nylon.

Brushwork and texture. In this small format painting, the drawing was executed entirely in color and the brushwork applied with the *alla prima* technique. Without a prelim-

inary sketch, the result appears fresh and spontaneous, since each brushstroke was applied resolutely, so as to be definitive. The contrast in the foreground is formed of a cool range of tones, including a few hints of color from other ranges. To attain a work of this nature, it is necessary to synthesize the rhythm of the composition by the colors and the brushstrokes.

A special vase. A simple vase of flowers can be turned into something very special. An interesting reflection may allow the artist to work with an unusual color range.

A unique urban landscape. Light and shadow form an urban landscape. The subject is developed with a daring color range, playing with the contrast between warm colors illumi-

nated by the sunlight and the cool colors of the buildings in shadow, to which hints of warm colors have been added to represent the warm reflections.

Another example of cool-warm contrast. This wicker stool was painted with a bright red-orange application in the most illuminated zones to capture the

intense light coming through the window, while the parts in shadow were painted with a range of blues. This produces a striking contrast and makes the stool appear to emerge from the canvas. By comparison, the middle ground, containing the radiator and window, was given less contrast. Finally, the background was not painted with the same

amount of detail as the foreground and middle ground. The less intense light of the background gradually increases as it penetrates the room. The shadows are the result of two light sources: that from outside and the interior's electric lighting.

Reverberation. It is important to study light. The aim of this fast sketch was to capture the special light of a summer afternoon. The sunlight was intense and it appeared to float within an atmosphere of shimmering light. The atmosphere was overwhelming and everything appeared very hazy.

The fluidity of the brushwork, together with a dirty palette, allowed the artist to capture the scene. The shadows provide the contrast in this range of neutral colors.

A harmonizing element. The light and the red curtain lend the

subject a suitable color harmony. The small red merry-go-round makes for an interesting contrast between the red zone and the gray-white zone. The red warms the shadows of the car in the foreground and produces fascinating effects.

PAINTING GRASS

Usefulness of Preliminary Sketches

Here you can see two studies of grass. They are preliminary sketches for a large painting of a figure lying in a meadow reading.

The intention was not to paint the meadow as such, but to *take inspiration* from it to produce a *creative* work in its composition and color.

Each sketch shows one pre-dominant "temperature":

A clear cool tendency (1). The basic colors used are cadmium yellow lemon, yellow ochre, rose madder, emerald green, permanent green, ultramarine blue, and a little white.

A warmer tendency (2). This palette includes cadmium yellow lemon and cadmium yellow medium, cadmium red, rose madder, emerald green, permanent green, cobalt blue, ultramarine blue, and much more white than palette 1.

Both studies were planned to be used together. The first is more detailed, as you can see in the foreground. The other shows less contrast and intensity and represents the grass seen in a more distant plane.

Our intention was also to coordinate the palettes of each sketch to obtain a harmonic combination of them later.

Sketches of Grass

1

Sketch of grass painted with mainly green, blue, and violet combinations to create tonal and color contrasts.

2

This second colored sketch, to be studied with the first, focuses more on the aspect of color, and follows the rule of reducing contrasts in more distant planes.

Observing Grass

Let us imagine it is daytime and we have before us a meadow of wild grass. This apparently banal subject is a simple yet significant exercise. Why?

How do we approach the structure of a painting? By balancing the areas that comprise this structure, bearing in mind that they are going to form part of a whole.

Let us closely study this meadow.

Photographs of a patch of grass: cool (left); warmer (right).

Grass: Color and Characteristics

Grass's own, natural color is green. Each stem, each blade, every species is a different green. Grass is not characterized by a single green but by an infinite number of greens. In addition to this, the grass will appear "warmer" depending on the type of light that strikes it: a bluish cool when in shadow; very warm when seen in spring under strong sunlight.

Synthesis

Each blade of grass poses a mini-problem. Each blade is exposed to the light, has its own shadow and can also cast a shadow on the earth or on surrounding blades. It would be madness to attempt to paint each single blade of grass from nature. A good idea is to paint it in groups, as suggested by the subject itself: clumps of grass.

Looking through squinted eyes helps to situate the different overall tones of the grass.

Rhythm

Studying grass from nature is an excellent way of learning its rhythms: how the blades sag under their own weight, the alternating upright and fallen blades....Grass is inspiring.

The artist can paint it just as it is, or offer the spectator her own composition, her own rhythm. This is an interesting exercise because it allows the artist to establish a direct relationship between the brushwork and the motion of the grass.

Distinguishing Between Planes

In the foreground, the grass appears in detail, with well-defined brushstrokes; this detail, however, fades as it stretches away into the distance.

The color of the grass loses contrast and intensity the farther away the grass is.

Enlargements in which you can compare the different degrees of concentration and contrast: foreground (left); most distant plane (right).

COLORING THE CANVAS

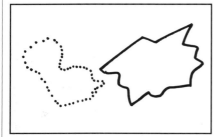
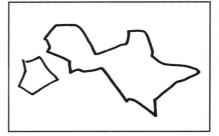

Diagram: centers of interest in each of the studies. They are located in the golden section, which are the areas of the painting on which the spectator focuses.

The Background Color

The brushwork representing the grass is set against a background.

This background should be painted so as to create a contrast with the grass itself.

Factors that affect this background are:

1. The influence of the color of the ground.

2. An atmosphere with a blue tendency in which the intensity of the light fades.

3. An atmosphere with a warm tendency, due to the phenomenon of reverberation under strong sunlight.

4. The influence of the green grass and its complementary color, rose madder.

5. Neutral colors (obtained by complementary colors) can be used for painting the background, as they are the perfect counterbalance to the saturated, intense tones of the grass.

6. In short, there is a wide range of colors that can be used to paint the background.

Cropping

In these studies of grass, we have blocked out the areas of greatest intensity of light or interest. Overall tonal areas can be established. For these areas, the right relationship between the background and the brushwork representing the grass must be found.

The Preliminary Colors

The preliminary colors should be lean. In each of these studies, there are areas that are well defined. For the coolest grass, a bluish green, blue, or bluish violet can be used, which can be mixed using ultramarine blue, cobalt blue, and rose madder, together with emerald green. The grass with the warmest tones requires a background painted in very pale blues or violets, together with neutral ochre

Observation

One method for painting the background that produces excellent results is as follows: The paint is removed while still wet, using a cotton cloth to create the right texture for the second stage of the brushwork. As you can see in the example, the areas in which the grass will be painted are clearly marked out.

Marks left after removing the wet paint using a cotton cloth wrapped around a finger.

Tonal Areas

For both studies, you should consult this work to see how the color ranges are used. For this stage, violets, blue-violets, blues, blue-greens, and yellow-greens are all useful colors. The artist should remember that the painting can be harmonized by correctly using tones, so the white in color mixtures must be used carefully. Harmonization can also be achieved through the use of temperature. As greens and blues are cool colors (pages

Tonal areas in black and white, taken from both studies of the grass.

Both studies shown together. Color enlargement of the dotted square.

66 and 67), the interesting point of this exercise is how to warm the colors of the grass; for this technique, see pages 64, 65, 68, and 69.

Chromatic Balance

This composition is a fine example of how all the areas of a painting should be balanced in color, tone, and intensity. Changes in color and contrasts should be used for a purpose: because they represent a transition from an illuminated area to one in shadow, for example, or because the grass is so distant that its shape is indistinguishable—only the color and tone can be seen.

This transition from one area to another is achieved by:

a) using red madder and violet mixtures in backgrounds.

b) using yellowish greens and olive greens, light in tone for the brushstrokes and lines that represent the grass.

PAINTING *ALLA PRIMA*

When painting landscapes, it is useful to apply a very quick painting technique in which the picture is finished in a single session: this is known as painting *alla prima*.

A canvas that has already been primed and left to dry, using greenish ochre acrylic paint (see example) or a lean layer of the same color in oils is an excellent foundation for painting a landscape, such as the one shown in the photograph. When you plan to paint quick landscapes, it is advisable to have small canvases already prepared, primed in neutral colors. Greens are very good base colors for landscapes containing a lot of vegetation.

This priming allows you to paint over in oil, applying thick, opaque layers of paint and even impasto work. Thus, in a single session the work reaches the level of a definitive painting.

Painting Impressions

Alla prima painting is a form of painting "impressions." This technique, as its name indicates, was fashionable among the Impressionist painters, who sought to capture moments of light and color. In this technique, only essential detail is included, as this style does not lend itself to excessively detailed work. It is best to mix the colors on the palette and paint the canvas by areas, so that the color mixtures on the canvas are well thought out and the colors do not interfere with each other.

A Palette for Painting This Sketch

You need the following colors: titanium white, cadmium yellow lemon, cadmium yellow medium,

Landscape photograph: Escornalbou

Color sample for priming the canvas.

Photograph of painting by M. Braunstein: Escornalbou.

Quick pencil sketch on paper.

yellow ochre, cadmium red, rose madder, permanent green, emerald green, cobalt, and ultramarine blue.

A small pencil sketch will help to situate the masses.

Now let's see how to paint the numbered areas.

The Sky

1. The sky is much darker at the top: A good amount of white is mixed with a little cobalt blue and a touch of ultramarine blue. The curvature of the sky is captured by lightening the color gradually as it stretches into the distance. The lightest area is painted with a little cobalt blue and a small touch of cadmium yellow lemon. Certain areas are left unpainted for the clouds.

2. Clouds can be painted in the following way: They are first painted in white and then the artist gently rubs his finger around the silhouette of the cloud to soften the outline and blend it into the sky.

3. The treetops on the left are painted by using the finger to blend the greens and the color of

4. A lot of white is needed for this section, plus a little cadmium red and a little cadmium yellow lemon. This mixture can also be used for the illuminated rocks below.

5. A lot of white is again necessary for this area, together with a little cadmium yellow lemon and a little yellow ochre.

6. This area requires a lot of white, a little yellow ochre, and a slight touch of cobalt blue.

7. Yellow ochre and a little ultramarine blue with a touch of white is mixed for this area. The result should be darker than the color in 6.

8. White with yellow ochre, cadmium red, and white by itself. This mixture is darkened, the red becoming carmine, while a little ultramarine blue is added for the darkest area.

Distinguishing Between Greens

In this landscape, the vegetation can be divided into roughly four areas:

A. The underbrush in front of the houses is a strong ochre color, the color of grass burnt dry by the sun.

B. The trees on the lower right are a dark green with golden and reddish hues that lend them volume.

C. The vegetation visible between the houses on the right is green with a strong blue tendency in comparison to the rest of the landscape.

D. There are darker greens that contrast with the more golden greens. This area appears darker than the underbrush.

The basic color that harmonizes the greens is yellow ochre. Here are the greens, from the darkest to the lightest:
- emerald green with yellow ochre and a little ultramarine blue.
- emerald green with yellow ochre.
- permanent green with yellow ochre.
- and last, white is added to lighten the tone.

As a general rule, a little cadmium red is added when a reddish ochre hue is desired.

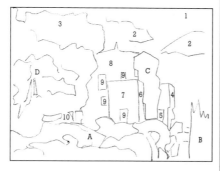

Photograph of numbered sketch.

the sky and clouds. This suggests the light that filters through the sparser foliage of the tree.

The Houses

Here we need to distinguish the walls using different colors and lighting.

The buildings on the right are the most brightly illuminated. In the middle there is a light area, while the most distant wall is pink.

The house at the front tends toward a creamy, grayish ochre and the right wall has a lighter tone. The building in the background has a pinkish hue, becoming darker in the area of the cast shadow. Mix the colors corresponding to the numbered sketch.

9. The doors and windows are painted with overlapping brushwork as a softer contrast is required for details in the background. The first brushstroke should be a mixture of yellow ochre, cobalt blue, and white. The second, applied over wet, is a mixture of yellow ochre, rose madder, and white.

10. The strokes of light colors indicating the wash are painted at the end, when the painting is considered balanced. These consist of just a few brushstrokes of neutral white, yellow ochre, and cobalt blue. They are applied onto the dry, primed surface thickly, impasto style, using a palette knife.

Summary

We have attempted to achieve a final, gently balanced result without too sharp a contrast. This produces an overall impression of the landscape. The dominant color of this quick sketch is a golden tone that unifies all the color mixtures. The keys to this *alla prima* painting are the yellow ochre color that harmonizes the whole, along with the simple use of color for the buildings and the vegetation, in addition to the technique for painting skies and clouds.

There are techniques that can soften the contrasts of the vegetation, such as using the finger to blend the wet colors or using the frottage technique of rubbing a dry brush over a textured surface and letting the underlying colors show through.

GLOSSARY

Basic colors (primary and secondary). In subtractive chromatic-synthesis, primary colors are yellow, magenta, and cyan blue, while secondary colors are red, green, and dark blue. (Primary colors are sometimes called fundamental colors, while secondary colors are sometimes known as binary, or mixed colors.)

Blue. This is the color perceived by the human eye and produced by light radiation at wavelengths between 460 and 482 nanometers.

Chromatics. Scientific study of colors with reference to hue and saturation. In current chromatics, the term light-colors has become obsolete, although it is still a valid term for the artist as it enables him to understand the environment in which he works.

Color. Color is an attribute of normal human vision, characterized by multi-cellular reception of light (by means of rods and cones). In painting, this term is applied to the attributes of light and objects. Color is a visual sensation comprising luminosity, hues, and saturation (or tone). "A painter's colors are not those of a physician"; that is, there are no hard and fast rules dictating what colors an artist should use. Although light is essential for both, the artist uses materials that produce optical effects by means of texture and behavior, via a process of subject selection during the creative process.

Color harmony. In oil painting, harmony is based on establishing an association between the colors. There are traditionally two methods of harmonization:
a) A general background color, painted over wet or dry with other colors, helps to harmonize them.
b) A small amount of the color chosen as the dominant tone can be added to all the mixtures on the palette, creating a harmonious effect.

Color theory. Name given to the science of color until 1931.

Complementary colors. In practice, a mixture of complementary pigment colors (that is, a mixture of a primary color with a secondary color that does not contain the former) produces a dirty color with a grayish tendency. Pairs of complementary colors are: red and green, yellow and violet, blue and orange. Optically, a color is heightened by the proximity of its complementary color. Two adjacent colors enrich each other with their respective complementary colors. For example, two warm colors (red and orange) are "cooled" by the color produced by their complementary colors.

Contrast. Contrast is defined as the opposition between two colors, divided into tonal contrast, color contrast, and contrast of temperatures.

Expression. The capacity to communicate emotion by means of artistic forms, using pictorial techniques which may even be exaggerated.

Glaze. A transparent layer of paint.

Highlights. Physical quality referring to the luminous intensity of the radiation.

Hue. Each radiation of a certain, dominant wavelength is perceived by the human eye and termed differently. Bluish purple: from 380 to 390 nms; blue-purple: 390 and 494 nms; dark blue: 460 to 482 nms; cyan blue (light blue): 482 to 487 nms; green: from 498 to 530 nms; purple: from 492 to 567 nms; yellow tending toward green: 575 to 580 nms; orange: from 585 to 620 nms; red: from 620 to 770 nms. All this information is summarized in the spectrum band of white light.

Impressionism. The Impressionists used a form of realism that imitated the impressions received by the eye by juxtaposing colors to create vibrant light.

Luminosity. A psychological concept based on the assumption that energy gives off light.

Nanometer (nm). Unit of length equivalent to one billionth of a meter; abbreviated as nm.

Neutral color. A neutral color is defined as a color obtained by mixing two colors that are complementaries, in unequal proportions, with or without white. Note: there are three primary colors in all neutral colors (with or without white).

Ostwald, Wilhelm. German scientist and philosopher who created a system for ordering standard colors with a psychophysical basis (1918). In 1931, Ostwald published his *Science and Color*.

Photo-reception. The light absorbed by pigments in the human retina in a photochemical reaction, producing a stimulus that is the origin of sight itself. This occurs by means of electromagnetic energy with electrical discharges that provoke nerve impulses that stimulate the brain's cortex.

Pigment. A coloring material in the form of powder, used to make paint.

Purity. Psycho-physical attribute of standard colors measured by the degree of saturation and intensity.

Red. This is the color perceived by the human eye and produced by light radiation at wavelengths between 680 and 770 nanometers.

Sketch. A drawing or painting not intended to be a definitive work, but rather one that precedes the finished work. It is generally painted from nature, to allow the artist to become better acquainted with the subject before representing it.

Spectrum. Dispersion of radiation characterized by its different wavelengths. White light as perceived by a normal human eye has a wavelength that ranges from 380 to 770 nanometers.

Standard color. Light-color, pigment-color, color in a figurative sense. The standard colors that reach the human eye have different wavelengths. Standard pigments are produced industrially.

Subtractive chromatic-synthesis. This is based on the diminishing effect of pigments. The chromatic-synthesis of primary subtractive pairs (subtractive synthesis) produces standard colors that are less intense than their primary colors.

White light. Light detected by the human eye. Its wavelength ranges from 380 to 770 nanometers.

Yellow. This is the color perceived by the human eye and produced by light radiation at wavelengths between 575 and 580 nanometers.

Editor in chief: María Fernanda Canal
Editor: Tomàs Ubach
Editorial Assistant/Illustration Archivist:
Mª Carmen Ramos

Text and Coordination: Mercedes Braunstein
Exercises: Mercedes Braunstein
Series Graphic Design: Toni Inglès
Book Graphic Design: José Carlos Escobar
Photography: Studio Nos & Soto

Production Director: Rafael Marfil
Production: Manel Sánchez

Original title of the book in Spanish:
Mezcla de colores: 2. Óleo

© Copyright Parramón Ediciones, S.A.,
World Rights

Published by Parramón Ediciones, S.A.
Empresa del Grupo Editorial Norma
de América Latina
www.parramon.com

Translated by Michael Brunelle and
Beatriz Cortabarría

ISBN: 978-84-342-3335-5

Printed in Spain